BRITISH RAILWAYS

PAST and PRESENT
Special
THE
TARKA TRAIL

SOUTHERN RAILWAY.

(12/28)   (787)

FROM WATERLOO TO

BARNSTAPLE JUNC.

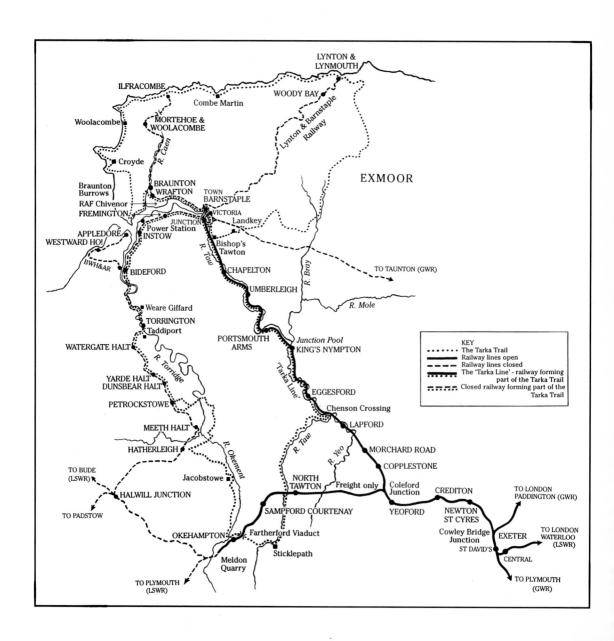

LYNTON &
LYNMOUTH

ILFRACOMBE
Combe Martin
WOODY BAY

Woolacombe
MORTEHOE &
WOOLACOMBE

R. Caen

Lynton & Barnstaple Railway

EXMOOR

Croyde

Braunton
Burrows
BRAUNTON
WRAFTON
TOWN
BARNSTAPLE

RAF Chivenor
FREMINGTON
VICTORIA
Landkey

APPLEDORE
WESTWARD HO!
JUNCTION
Power Station
INSTOW

R. Bray

R. Taw

Bishop's
Tawton

BWH&AR
BIDEFORD
CHAPELTON
TO TAUNTON (GWR)

UMBERLEIGH

Weare Giffard
R. Mole

TORRINGTON
Taddiport

WATERGATE HALT
PORTSMOUTH
ARMS
Junction Pool
KING'S NYMPTON

R. Torridge

'Tarka Line'

YARDE HALT
DUNSBEAR HALT
EGGESFORD

PETROCKSTOWE
Chenson Crossing

MEETH HALT
LAPFORD

R. Okement
R. Taw
R. Yeo
MORCHARD ROAD

HATHERLEIGH
COPPLESTONE

TO BUDE
(LSWR)
Jacobstowe
NORTH
TAWTON
Freight only
Coleford
Junction
CREDITON
TO LONDON
PADDINGTON (GWR)

HALWILL JUNCTION
YEOFORD
NEWTON
ST CYRES
TO LONDON
WATERLOO
(LSWR)

TO PADSTOW
SAMPFORD COURTENAY

OKEHAMPTON
Fartherford Viaduct
Cowley Bridge
Junction
EXETER

Sticklepath
ST DAVID'S
CENTRAL

Meldon
Quarry
TO PLYMOUTH
(GWR)

TO PLYMOUTH
(LSWR)

KEY
········· The Tarka Trail
━━━━━ Railway lines open
─ ─ ─ Railway lines closed
The 'Tarka Line' - railway forming part of the Tarka Trail
Closed railway forming part of the Tarka Trail

BRITISH RAILWAYS

PAST and PRESENT
Special
THE
TARKA TRAIL

A nostalgic journey by train, foot and cycle through beautiful North Devon

Terry Gough

Past and Present

Past & Present Publishing Ltd

First published in March 1995

British Library Cataloguing in Publication Data

A catalogue record for this book is available from the British Library

ISBN 1 85895 078 3

Past & Present Publishing Ltd
Unit 5
Home Farm Close
Church Street
Wadenhoe
Peterborough PE8 5TE
Tel/fax (0832) 720440

Printed and bound in Great Britain

Title page The author was issued with this traditional pre-printed card ticket on his first visit to the Tarka Line, on 6 September 1953. In the early 1980s these began to be replaced by a variety of tickets with destinations printed on demand. The BR ticket for the same journey was issued almost exactly 40 years after the first.

Below A Southern Railway excursion advertisement. Note that Bideford to Hatherleigh is only available on Tuesdays despite a daily service being provided. Tuesday was (and still is) market day.

Opposite A plaque commemorating the opening of the Tarka Trail displayed at Bideford station. *TG*

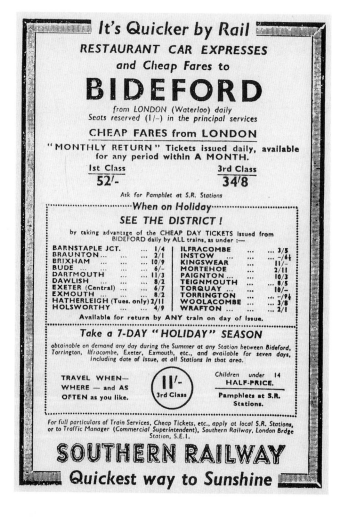

CONTENTS

In the early days of diesel operation, trains displayed a headcode, of little value to passengers but intended to inform railway staff. Here '2C79' signifies the type of train (2), the operating area (C), and the route (79); it is an Ilfracombe train leaving King's Nympton in the summer of 1967.

Present-day King's Nympton from the same point shows a Barnstaple-bound train consisting of Class '153' No 153355 passing through the station on 27 August 1993. *Both TG*

INTRODUCTION

'Among the quiet hills and meadows in the middle of Devon, this small train of three spruce coaches was the only moving object, and its harmless racket the only sound.'

from *The Kingdom by the Sea* by Paul Theroux

The Tarka Trail is a long distance path in North Devon completed in 1992, and giving visitors the opportunity to enjoy the area without the intrusion of the motor car. It is centred on Barnstaple, from which it describes a figure of eight, with its extremities at Lynton and Okehampton. Different parts of the Trail can be covered by rail, by foot and by cycle and in total it covers 180 miles of some of the most beautiful countryside in the United Kingdom.

The various elements of the Trail are not all new and a significant part makes use of railway lines. Indeed, Barnstaple is reached by train from Exeter, a route named the 'Tarka Line' by British Rail in 1990, and from Eggesford to Barnstaple the line actually constitutes part of the Trail.

For visitors coming by car the North Devon Link Road from Tiverton offers a quick route to Barnstaple. However, there are other more attractive routes from the east over Exmoor, and from Exeter on the former main road that runs parallel to the railway line and the River Taw for most of its length.

Closed railway lines also form part of the Trail, including part of the Barnstaple to Ilfracombe line. South-west of Barnstaple the Trail uses the line that followed the River Torridge to Bideford and Torrington. Beyond Torrington the trackbed of the North Devon & Cornwall Junction Light Railway (NDCJLR) is used almost to Hatherleigh. Further south the Trail meets the railway briefly at Okehampton (on what was the Exeter to Plymouth main line) and again near North Tawton on the same line.

Long-established public footpaths make up other parts of the Tarka Trail, for example that between Barnstaple and Lynton, which crosses the old railway line from Taunton to Barnstaple near Landkey, then climbs Exmoor to join the Two Moors Way for the walk to Lynton. The Two Moors Way, as the name implies, links Exmoor and Dartmoor and ends at Ivybridge, more than 100 miles from the North Devon coast; it passes close to Morchard Road station on the Exeter to Barnstaple line. At Lynton the terminus of the closed narrow-gauge Lynton & Barnstaple Railway can still be seen.

Elsewhere the Trail uses minor roads, particularly where there is no public footpath and it has not proved possible to obtain permission to use privately owned land. Much of the Trail between Petrockstowe and Okehampton falls into this category.

The part of the Trail suitable for cyclists is restricted mainly to the former railway lines, which provide an excellent way for people of all ages to enjoy the area in complete safety and without the same level of exertion necessary for other parts of the Trail. Horse riding is permitted (at least experimentally) along the former railway line from Torrington to Petrockstowe.

Much has been published on the area covered by the Trail, by far the best known being the book *Tarka the Otter* by Henry Williamson, first published in 1927 and frequently reprinted in both hardback and paperback. There are also many books on local history, and those that are out of print are available in public libraries and the North Devon Record Office in Barnstaple. Some address a particular aspect (such as Chivenor Airfield), whilst others are of a more general nature and give more of an overview for the visitor. An example is the Warner *Red Guide,* which gives information on many of the towns and villages through which the Trail passes.

A few books discuss the railway history of North Devon, with the building of the Taw Valley Railway between Barnstaple and Fremington, the arguments over the merits of the broad and standard gauges, establishment of a network throughout North Devon, and its ultimate decline in recent years. The short life of the narrow-gauge Lynton & Barnstaple Railway is also recorded in several books. There was also a narrow-gauge mineral railway in the Torrington and Petrockstowe area, which was later absorbed into one of the last railway lines to be built in the United Kingdom. This was the line from Torrington to Halwill Junction, opened in 1925.

North Devon has seen many changes since *Tarka the Otter* was written. Some of these changes have been brought about by forces external to North Devon, in particular the desire of people from the more crowded parts of the United Kingdom to experience another lifestyle and environment. There is inevitably a conflict of interests, but, despite the economic pressure to attract visitors to North Devon, the environment has suffered far less than other once isolated parts of the country. Industrial development has also taken place, and the coming of the canal, then the railway, did much to enhance both tourism and industry; the latter is based mostly on local resources, especially related to farming.

The decline of the railways has been brought about mainly by the ever-increasing availability of the motor vehicle and by the demands of local industry to use what was perceived as more convenient road transport. Despite the shift from rail to road by both passengers and freight, most roads in North Devon do not have a significantly greater carrying capacity than in the immediate past decades. Although Barnstaple has had a succession of peripheral routes designed to avoid the town centre, and some of the villages have bypasses, most towns and villages are still immediately recognisable from photographs taken in Henry Williamson's time. The vast majority also remain unspoilt.

Similarly with the countryside; although hosting an ever-increasing number of visitors and suffering from the effects of both land and water pollution, the much greater awareness in recent years of the need to protect and preserve our inheritance has led to an increasing respect for the environment. Hence the birth of the Tarka Project, under the auspices of the relevant District Councils, the County Council and the Countryside Commission. The Project has three main objectives:

> to protect and enrich the wildlife, natural beauty and special character of North Devon
> to encourage public enjoyment and understanding of the area
> to promote tourism and recreation

The choice of name for the project was clearly appealing to the emotions and consciences of the many people who would be familiar with *Tarka the Otter.* Such visitors could thus see that they were welcome to visit North Devon, they could contribute economically to the area, and with common sense and sensitivity enjoy the beauty without jeopardising the special nature of the environment for future generations. There is also a North Devon Rail Users' Group, formed in 1978 to encourage the use of the Barnstaple to Exeter railway for both passenger and freight transport.

This book has been written as a photographic reflection on the changes that have occurred at the places served by the railway and which now form part of the Tarka Trail. Its origins began unwittingly as a result of my first visit to North Devon in 1953, when I set myself the objective of seeing how far I could reach (and return) by rail in one day from my home in Surrey. The destination was Barnstaple, but in this I failed. In the event, late running of my train meant that to avoid missing the last train of the day back home, I had to turn round at Umberleigh.

Since that introduction to North Devon I have visited the area many times, in my early years by bicycle as part of my annual grand tour of the South West, joined after a few years by a young lady. Later in life the family holidays were spent camping between Barnstaple and Ilfracombe, admittedly travelling from home by car. Life has now turned almost full circle, the children are themselves adults and the young lady and I now come to North Devon with our bicycles to enjoy the Tarka Trail.

Although this book concentrates on the railways of the Trail, it is not a book exclusively for the railway enthusiast. Neither is it a book for historians, despite the many comparisons of 'past' with 'present'. It is also not a guidebook, as there is already a helpful book (*The Tarka Trail, A Walkers' Guide*) describing the Trail. It is simply for all those who love North Devon, whether visitor or local, and who wish to enjoy comparing the past with the present, whatever mode of transport they may be using. I hope that this book will complement the *Walkers' Guide* and that as you reach each place the photographs will help you imagine what it was like so many years ago.

While most people visit the Tarka Trail during the summer months, the Trail has a special and different beauty in each of the four seasons. Unlike Dartmoor, North Devon does not appear bleak even in the depths of winter. The visitor will, however, find that the Trail takes on a completely different character, apart from being much quieter. Walking, cycling or travelling by train in spring reveals much that is not visible in the summer when new foliage blocks the view; this is particularly so on the section from Landcross (south of Bideford) to just beyond Torrington. The Trail is for all seasons, as reflected in the colour photographs taken at the same point in summer and winter.

Cycles can be hired at several points on the Trail, including Eggesford, Barnstaple, Braunton, Instow and Bideford. Cycles can also be taken on the trains, although space is limited and advanced booking is advisable but not mandatory.

In steam days there were regular through trains from Waterloo, in addition to local trains starting from Exeter. After the Second World War a Pullman train, the 'Devon Belle', was introduced, running from Waterloo to Ilfracombe, but it only lasted seven years, being withdrawn in 1954. Much longer lived was the 'Atlantic Coast Express', which the Southern Railway introduced in 1926. This had portions for the East Devon resorts, Plymouth, North Cornwall and North Devon, and ran on a regular basis (other than during the war) until the end of the summer season of 1964. That year marked the end of through trains from Waterloo, and the introduction of diesels. Trains then ran between Exeter St David's and Ilfracombe with connecting services for Torrington at Barnstaple Junction.

The Beeching Report of 1963 recommended closure of all intermediate stations between Exeter and Barnstaple, except Crediton, Lapford and Eggesford. In the event all stations are still open, although not all are served by all trains. In steam days an all-stations train took about 1½ hours from Exeter St David's to Barnstaple, a distance of 39 miles. The current diesel units on an all-stations service take 1¼ hours, and the fastest train, with only three intermediate stops, takes just under 1 hour.

For many years there was a basic weekday service of 10 trains in each direction per day. Following the introduction of diesel trains the number was gradually reduced until there were only seven trains. However, in the last few years 10 trains have been reinstated and in 1994 the best service for decades was introduced with 12 trains per day.

I have tried to maintain a transport theme throughout this book, and apart from railways I have included the motor bus and car, horse-drawn cart, aeroplane and, of course, the bicycle.

ACKNOWLEDGEMENTS

Most importantly I wish to record my thanks for support over so many years to the young lady on the bicycle, my wife Cynthia. She has accompanied me on all visits to obtain material for this book, in the course of which she has cycled many miles and spent hours in the North Devon Record Office searching the archives for suitable material. I thank her for her patience, support and encouragement. At the Record Office, we have received a great deal of help and advice from Bryony Harris, who also undertook the processing of all the photographs attributed to the Beaford Archive. She also commented on this manuscript. For all this I am most grateful.

I also gratefully acknowledge the various photographers who have provided material from their collections: Richard Casserley, Denis Cullum, Cyril Found, Chris Gammell, Lawrence Golden, Frank Hornby, Ronald Lumber, David Mitchell, Terry Nicholls, Bill Pryor, Dick Riley, Stuart Smallridge, John Smith (Lens of Sutton), Spencer Taylor and Alan Wilkinson, and to Stephen Knight for photographs taken by his grandfather, Mr R. L. Knight

I thank Derek Mercer who expertly printed all my own photographs from both 'past' and 'present' eras. I also thank the Committee members of the Bideford & Instow Railway Group for willingly giving access to their archive material, and Joy Slocombe, Curator of Ilfracombe Museum.

Finally I record my thanks to the various land-owners who have given me access to their property. In particular I thank the owners of Eggesford House, who were especially helpful in permitting access to their private estate which under normal circumstances is not open to visitors.

Terry Gough
Woking
February 1995

1
THE APPROACH TO NORTH DEVON

There were two railway routes to Barnstaple, the Great Western Railway (GWR) line from Taunton, which was opened in 1873, and the London & South Western Railway (LSWR) line from Exeter. The former, which ran through Dulverton and South Molton, had in steam days a bi-hourly service; there were also several through trains from London (Paddington) throughout the year. The decline of the line began in the late 1950s, and towards the end of its life services were reduced to a handful of local trains. The GWR station at Barnstaple closed to passengers in 1960 and trains were diverted to the ex-LSWR station at Barnstaple Junction, then the line from Taunton closed completely in 1966. Present-day motorists, the majority unwittingly, follow the course of this line for much of its route, by virtue of approaching Barnstaple along the North Devon Link Road.

The LSWR line to Barnstaple has a complex history, which is well recorded in a number of books (see the Bibliography). Trains ran regularly from Waterloo to Exeter Queen Street (later renamed Central), and points further west. In summer months many of these trains were packed to capacity with holidaymakers, and on Saturdays additional trains were provided. The fall in the number of railway passengers from the late 1950s also had a dramatic effect on these services, so that by the time the use of steam traction was coming to an end, so were the through services from London to North Devon. The last regular through trains from Waterloo ran in the summer of 1964. The complete abandonment of all North Devon lines and the ex-LSWR main line to Plymouth became a serious consideration. In the event the North Devon line is still open for passengers as far as Barnstaple (the 'Tarka Line') and the Plymouth line as far as Meldon Quarry (just beyond Okehampton) for stone trains. There are still services from both Paddington and Waterloo to Exeter, with the former being the quicker and giving much better connections at Exeter St David's for the Barnstaple trains.

However, the line from Waterloo is both the historically 'correct' way to connect with Barnstaple trains, and is by far the more scenically attractive route, passing over Salisbury Plain, along the Blackmoor Vale and through a succession of junction stations that used to serve branches to Dorset and East Devon towns, of which only the Exmouth branch survives. The LSWR main line has been managed successively by the Southern Railway, and the Southern and (west of Salisbury) the Western Regions of British Rail. It more recently became part of Network SouthEast and, from April 1994, has been operated by South West Trains.

Steam-hauled 12-coach trains from Waterloo to Exeter were once commonplace, but they gave way to shorter and shorter diesel locomotive-hauled trains as the railway lost its passengers to road transport. The increasing migration of holidaymakers to other European countries also played a significant part. The line declined in importance and could well have closed, had it not been for a change in policy within railway management and pressure from com-

London and South Western Ry.

787

TO

EXETER (QUEEN ST.)

SOUTHERN RAILWAY.

(1/34)

(787)

FROM WATERLOO TO

EXETER CENTRAL

munities along the route to revitalise it. Several stations between Salisbury and Exeter, closed in the 1960s, have been reopened and the service has been much improved in the last few years. In 1993 new trains were introduced on all Waterloo to Exeter services, and further improvements in frequency were made in 1994, so the old LSWR line remains an ideal route by which to reach the Tarka Trail.

The present-day visitor arriving at Exeter Central will be struck by the size of the station in comparison to its services. It was opened by the Southern Railway in 1933 on the site of the LSWR Queen Street station, and was the point at which many of the express trains from London were divided, with parts for North Devon, North Cornwall and Plymouth. It was also the starting point for many local trains heading both east and west. The branch line trains to Exmouth also started here. There was a local goods yard and carriage sidings adjacent to the station, as well as much larger yards and engine sheds at Exmouth Junction 1¼ miles to the east.

The station buildings remain superficially unchanged, although much has been let for non-railway use, the track layout has been simplified and the goods yard and carriage sidings closed. Trains no longer divide here and services from Waterloo usually continue only as far

as the next station at Exeter St David's. The Exmouth branch trains still run and a very frequent service is provided; in addition there are a few morning and evening local trains that run to Honiton and Yeovil Junction. There are, of course, also the Tarka Line trains operated by Regional Railways, which start either here or come from Exmouth.

The line between Exeter Queen St and Exeter St David's was opened in 1862. Immediately beyond the western end of the LSWR station the railway line makes

What a welcome to the West Country! This is the 'Atlantic Coast Express' from Waterloo arriving at Exeter Central station during a downpour in midsummer 1960. The engine is 'West Country' Class No 34108 *Wincanton*, built by British Railways in 1950 to a Southern Railway design. The following year this engine was rebuilt and its streamlined casing removed to give a more conventional appearance. The engine to the right has just arrived with a train from Exmouth.

The new image is represented by a South Western Turbo train of Class '159', which were introduced exclusively for the Waterloo and Exeter services in 1993 to replace ageing diesel locomotives and coaches. This is No 159015 on the 12.35 from Waterloo on 5 September 1994. *Both TG*

one of the steepest descents of a main line in the country at a gradient of 1 in 37, made more challenging by incorporating a tunnel and a very tight curve, culminating in the junction with the GWR main line at St David's. A day spent at this location in steam days was fascinating, as a succession of trains tackled the bank.

The 16.21 Exeter Central to Barnstaple and Torrington train descends to St David's behind 'Battle of Britain' Class No 34110 *66 Squadron* on 12 August 1960. Climbing the bank is sister engine No 34074 *46 Squadron* on the 14.20 from Ilfracombe. The stock in the carriage sidings, which includes a restaurant car, will be attached to the latter, thus forming a 10-coach train for the journey to Waterloo. There are other carriage sidings to the right, and the station is immediately beyond the road bridge; the end of the down platform is just visible.

The 1980s scene shows that the carriage sidings have made way for a builders' merchant. A Barnstaple-bound train consisting of just three coaches descends to St David's on 3 April 1986. These first-generation British Rail diesel multiple units (DMUs) were used on most local trains in the West of England. *Both TG*

Watching a train climb the bank was impressive both to see and hear, particularly as it burst into the open from the tunnel. The heavier trains had at least one banking engine attached to the rear for the ascent and sometimes a second engine on the front as well. The heaviest trains were those conveying stone from Meldon Quarry near Okehampton, and on 12 August 1960 one such train was hauled by BR Standard Class '3MT' No 82025 and Class 'N' No 31844.

Meldon Quarry is still open, but stone trains no longer use this route to South East England, but reverse at Exeter Riverside yard (near St David's) and use the former GWR line. The Waterloo trains still pound up the bank, however, although to a very different sound; that emitted by the diesel engine. Until 1993 all Waterloo trains were hauled by diesel locomotives, such as this Class '50', No 50017 *Royal Oak*, which is working the 12.20 to Waterloo in the summer of 1986. *Both TG*

On emerging from the western end of the tunnel the rail traveller is treated to a rooftop view of the houses in Bonhay Road and the River Exe beyond. The present St David's station is the third on this site and was built by the GWR in 1914. It is almost unique in that trains from London regularly arrive from opposite directions; the only other example in the South West was Plymouth North Road until the closure of the LSWR route via Okehampton. Another feature is the sight of two trains leaving from the same platform almost simultaneously in opposite directions.

Dual occupancy of Platform 1 on 26 May 1987. Class '142' railbus No 142019 has just arrived on the 11.45 from Exmouth, to trap the 12.18 to Waterloo hauled by Class '50' No 50040 *Centurion*. The Barnstaple train in Platform 3 will also leave at 12.18, and is formed of another of the Class '142' railbuses known as 'Skippers', introduced amidst great publicity a few months earlier. Unfortunately the rigid wheelbase of these vehicles made them unsuitable for some of the lines in Devon and Cornwall and they were transferred away from the area in September 1987. In the intervening period the ageing diesel units introduced at the end of the steam era had been withdrawn for scrap, and for many months following the departure of the '142s' Tarka Line trains were worked by an assortment of diesel units or locomotives borrowed from other parts of the British Rail network.

This collection of old diesel units was not replaced until 1992 when new-generation units of Class '150' and others of similar design were allocated to all Devon and Cornwall branch lines. On 30 April 1994 platform 1 at St David's is occupied by Class '150' No 150230 forming a Paignton train. Behind is No 150269, recently arrived from Barnstaple, and on the left is Class '159' No 159005 leaving for the sidings after working the 10.35 from Waterloo. *Both TG*

2
THE 'TARKA LINE'

Immediately after leaving Exeter St David's trains pass the extensive freight yards of Exeter Riverside, where ballast wagons used on the stone trains from Meldon Quarry are often to be seen. Cowley Bridge, at the end of the yard, was the junction of the LSWR lines to Plymouth and Ilfracombe, and the GWR line to Bristol and beyond. Both railway companies used the same tracks between St David's and Cowley Bridge; plans for separate lines for each company never materialised. Cowley Bridge Junction still exists, but in simplified form, with the ex-LSWR line now being single track. Cowley Bridge also marks the confluence of the Rivers Exe and Yeo.

Right A 1980s poster advertising the railways of Devon. At that time the Barnstaple line was still referred to by its traditional name of the North Devon Line. *TG*

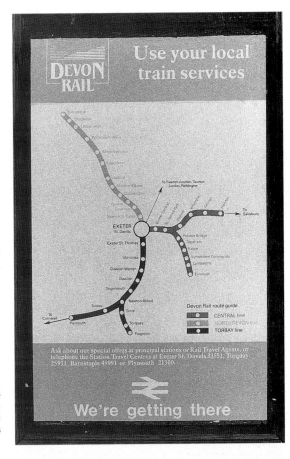

Below The line between Exeter St David's and Crediton was opened in 1851 and broad gauge trains were provided until 1892. A Barnstaple-bound train crosses the River Exe just beyond Cowley Bridge on 18 August 1989 and gives the traveller the first indications of the beauty of the countryside ahead. *TG*

Below Newton St Cyres has always been served only by local trains, the expresses passing through *en route* to Plymouth and Ilfracombe. Today the station is served by a small number of the 'Tarka Line' trains on request to the guard or by flagging down if one wishes to board. Several other stations on the 'Tarka Line' are served in this way, which is an admirable method of retaining a station that generates little revenue but performs a valuable social function. There was obviously double track through the station in earlier times as the abandoned down platform indicates. This is the view looking towards Exeter on 24 August 1989, with a Barnstaple train approaching the station. According to the winter 1993/4 timetable Newton St Cyres was in the unique position of having a Saturday-only train start here 'by request' and running as far as Umberleigh. A more careful study of the timetable revealed that the journey time from Newton St Cyres to Crediton was 42 minutes and to Umberleigh only 1 minute. British Rail subsequently issued an amendment claiming that this service was now discontinued, rather than admitting to misprints. *TG*

Below left Many of the 'Tarka Line' trains pass each other at Crediton, which is also the terminus for some trains from Exeter that run as part of a 'Park and Ride' scheme introduced in 1992. The old station buildings survive, although there are no booking facilities. The LSWR signal box at the west end of the station is still in use, controlling the barriers that have long since replaced the traditional railway level crossing gates. It is here that the drivers of Barnstaple-bound trains are given authority to proceed on the single line to the next passing place at Eggesford. This is undertaken manually using a modern version of the railway 'token'.

This is the view of Crediton from an Exeter-bound train on 3 August 1991, with Unit No 879 waiting clearance to leave for Barnstaple. This unit was made up from odd coaches of Classes '101' and '108' subsequent to the withdrawal of the 'Skippers'. *TG*

Bottom left The view from the footbridge at the west end of Crediton clearly shows two tracks, but these are operated as completely separate lines; the old down line is used exclusively by trains to and from Meldon Quarry. All 'Tarka Line' trains use the old up line, hence the need for single-line 'token' operation. On 12 August 1988 a stone train from Meldon hauled by Class '33' No 33039 approaches Crediton. There are several stone trains per day with corresponding return empty wagon workings. The times are variable, but there is usually one in each direction mid-morning, which together with the passenger trains to and from Exeter makes Crediton busy for short periods. *TG*

The line climbs gently beyond Cowley Bridge and passes through the stations of Newton St Cyres and Crediton. The latter town is worth a visit, and although not particularly attractive, with a main road passing through the centre, is of historical significance and was diocesan home of the bishop until this was transferred to Exeter in the 11th century.

Beyond Crediton the line climbs more steadily to Yeoford. The valley is still wide here as the river meanders from one side of the railway to the other. The Crediton to Barnstaple and Fremington line was opened three years after the Exeter to Crediton section, and was provided with broad gauge services until 1877. From 1863 standard gauge trains also ran between Exeter and Bideford. Through services between Exeter and Fremington began in 1855.

Yeoford, although serving a small community, was a busy interchange station until the end of the steam era. There were extensive sidings and much traffic in cattle, agricultural produce and equipment. Here also some of the expresses from Waterloo were divided, with one portion for North Devon and the other for Plymouth and North Cornwall. A visit on a dismal day in August 1960 found both passenger and freight activity. 'West Country' Class No 34002 *Salisbury* approaches the station on the 11.47 Exeter Central to Plymouth, while 'Battle of Britain' Class No 34056 *Croydon*, on an up freight train, waits in the bay.

All this has since been swept aside, as the same view in the 1980s shows. There are no sidings, no signals and only one platform, but at least the station is still open, although served only on request. The train is unit No P471 of Class '118' forming the 14.30 Barnstaple to Exeter St David's service. *Both TG*

The lines to Okehampton and Barnstaple diverged 1 mile beyond Yeoford at Coleford Junction, the former continuing west and the latter turning north-west. The first sod of the line from Yeoford to Okehampton was cut by the Countess of Portsmouth near here in 1864. A narrow road from Coleford village passes over the railway just west of the junction and gives good views of both lines, although foliage blocks the view of the 'Tarka Line' during the summer months. The junction was taken out in 1971, the two lines now running parallel to the junction at Crediton. Two Class '33s' have just passed the site of the junction on a train of empty wagons for Meldon on 12 August 1988. A bridge on the 'Tarka Line' can just be seen on the far left. *TG*

Copplestone is situated at the junction of the main roads to Barnstaple (A377) and Okehampton (A3072), and is the highest point on the railway from Exeter; hereafter the line falls all the way to Barnstaple. As the line approaches Copplestone it enters a cutting sandwiched between the northbound and southbound sections of the A377, here occupied by an afternoon Exeter to Barnstaple train in August 1988 consisting of unit No 956 of Class '108'. Copplestone has a place in railway history because it was in this cutting that the first sod of the North Devon Railway was cut in 1852 by the Hon Newton Fellowes, who became 4th Earl of Portsmouth (see page 28). *TG*

Old and new station signs at Copplestone. Although engineering works for double track between here and Umberleigh were undertaken, track was never laid and this section has always been single track with passing loops at intermediate stations. Coleford Junction to Copplestone was doubled in 1883. *TG*

Morchard Road station, built to serve the village of Morchard Bishop 2^1/$_2$ miles to the north-east, is, like all stations beyond Coleford Junction, close to the main A377 road. This has the advantage of easy access, but suffers from competition from road transport. Here is the station seen from Morchard Road bridge on 7 June 1994; the train is the 09.24 Exmouth to Barnstaple, which stops here by request. In common with most other stations on the line, Morchard Road was oil-lit, but the lamps were removed many years ago. More recently electric light has been installed, tactfully using lamps of the traditional style, although far taller than the originals. Morchard Road had a passing loop until 1964. *TG*

Between Morchard Road and Lapford, the road and railway are joined by a river, the second River Yeo in the county. The view looking north at this point is most attractive, although the river is hidden from view behind the trees to the right of the railway line. This point also marks the beginning of the meandering of the line to follow the river. Class '155' No 155315 forms an afternoon train from Barnstaple in July 1992. *TG*

Opposite Lapford station is close to the village and at one time the platforms for up and down trains were separated by the Exeter Road overbridge; all trains now use the former up platform. There is also a road bridge a few yards to the south of the station carrying a minor road to the village, and this gives a good view of the site of the down platform, which was in the loop; the main road bridge and station are in the background. A single-coach unit, No 153318, approaches the station on 27 July 1992.

The second view is of the same location, but the view of the loop and station is blocked by trees. This is not a 'past' photograph, but was taken subsequent to the previous one on the occasion of the first steam train on the 'Tarka Line' since the 1960s. This took place on 2 May 1994 to celebrate 150 years of railways at Exeter. The engine is Class '4MT' No 80080, which was built by British Railways in 1954. *Both TG*

Above An equally attractive view is obtained from the bridge at the other end of the station, which forms part of a public footpath, accessible from a gate near the far end of the platform. The Ambrosia cream factory, which provided local employment and traffic for the railway, was located adjacent to the station. Built in 1928, it closed in 1970 and the buildings are now used for other purposes, most importantly as a fertiliser distribution depot. Until 1993 fertiliser was delivered by rail; deliveries were usually in the early hours of the morning one day a week or as requested. All fertiliser is now brought by road, thus depriving the 'Tarka Line' of its last freight facility. Other traffic included animals (live and dead) and coal, and there is still a coal merchant operating from the goods yard. The wagons seen on the right formed almost the last fertiliser train to use Lapford, and were taken away a few days after this photograph was taken. *TG*

SOUTHERN RAILWAY.
(3/25)   Stock
                                               787
TO
LAPFORD

Left An unmade road crosses the railway at Chenson and this also constitutes a public footpath. Both old and modern notices warn of the dangers of crossing the railway without attention. The small modern triangular sign on the right portrays an InterCity 125 train, which is not as incongruous at it may appear. Very occasionally an InterCity train is used for excursions from Barnstaple, for example to Hampton Court and to York.

The significance of Chenson is that this is the point where the south-east section of the Tarka Trail is first encountered. The Trail has run parallel to the River Taw from North Tawton and Bondleigh to just below Chenson. At Chenson, instead of crossing the railway, it remains on the west side of the line until Eggesford station is reached. *TG*

Below left An excellent view of both the Tarka Trail (in the foreground) and the 'Tarka Line' can be had from Eggesford Garden Centre; similar views have been used by British Rail in its publicity material for the line. Cycles can be hired from the Garden Centre. The church is that of All Saints and was built for the benefit of the people of the Eggesford Estate. *TG*

Above With Eggesford Forest in the background, Class '150' No 150247 heads for Barnstaple on the 20 July 1992; the Tarka Trail lies to the left out of view. Eggesford Forest, much of which was once part of the Eggesford Estate whose history goes back to the 13th century, is owned by the Forestry Commission. There is a network of way-marked foot and cycle paths through the forest and several picnic areas. *TG*

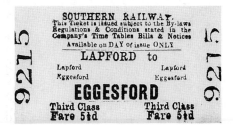

25

A reminder of the time when all trains were steam-hauled. 'West Country' Class No 34026 *Yes Tor* enters Eggesford on the 12.18 from Torrington to Waterloo on 3 August 1955.

Today Eggesford station is the only passing place for trains apart from Crediton. There is a level crossing at the station and the barriers are operated by the train crew, as the station is unstaffed. It is here also that the driver requires permission to proceed, and these two requirements usually result in a few minutes' wait at Eggesford, particularly if it is also necessary to pass a train heading in the opposite direction. Trains passing on 15 August 1987 are an Exeter-bound train hauled by Class '31' No 31406, seen from a northbound DMU. The main Exeter to Barnstaple road is immediately to the right

There is no village of Eggesford and the station is used by people from the nearby villages of Chawleigh and Chulmleigh and surrounding area. In the steam era there was a bus service to Torrington, but this ceased once private car ownership became commonplace. Amazingly, the service was reinstated in 1994 and one journey per week is made in each direction. *Denis Cullum/TG*

Above The age of steam was also the age of oil lamps, and this relic survived at Eggesford until the early 1980s. The lamp post originally had an oil lamp attached permanently to the cast brackets, but this was later replaced by a rather unattractive pole, from which a Tilley lamp would be hung by the porter at dusk. *TG*

Above right It was also the age of passengers with large amounts of luggage, and porters to assist. This trolley was photographed at Eggesford in 1985, but placed behind bars out of reach of intending users. *TG*

Right The telephoto lens gives a false sense of nearness of the church to the station. The position of the hut behind the 'Stop' sign was once occupied by a manually operated signal box. Built when the line was opened, the box was destroyed by flooding in the winter of 1967 and an ugly flat-roofed building replaced it until this was displaced in 1987 by the current means of controlling the barriers. *TG*

London and South Western Ry.
787
TO
EGGESFORD

The most famous landmark in the area was Eggesford House, built between 1820 and 1830 by the Hon Newton Fellowes, 4th Earl of Portsmouth. An earlier building of the same name located nearer the church was owned by the Copplestone family. Eggesford House remained with the Portsmouth family for three generations, and was sold by the 6th Earl in 1913. It then had a succession of owners, the last to occupy the house stripping it of much of the building material for use on his property elsewhere.

The house has remained in a state of dereliction ever since. In 1992 the Estate was sold and the present owners intend to restore part of the main house for their private use. *Beaford Archive/TG*

From Eggesford to Barnstaple the railway *is* the Tarka Trail, and for those visitors travelling from Exeter by train, this is an excellent introduction to the Trail. The intermediate stations, and particularly Umberleigh which has the better train service, are all good places to alight for a day's exploration of the surrounding countryside.

King's Nympton station is in one of the most attractive surroundings on the line and is located by a road junction known as Fortescue Cross. The station was originally named South Molton Road in an attempt to persuade travellers that the market town of the same name was close by; it was in fact 9 miles away. The GWR line to Barnstaple, which was opened much later, had its own station of South Molton only 1 mile from the town. Just after the nationalisation of the railways, South Molton Road was renamed King's Nympton after the nearest village 2½ miles away (and all uphill).

Above and below left King's Nympton station from the main road bridge looking towards Exeter on 22 August 1986. Class '142' No 142022 forms the 08.30 from Exmouth, which called at all stations from Exeter except Newton St Cyres. By this time the passing loop had been removed and only one platform was in use.

The same place five years later shows more change with the addition of a waiting shelter and further encroachment of trees. This is unit No 828 formed from odd coaches from Classes '101' and '108' necessitated by the withdrawal of the new Class '142' railbuses. *Both TG*

Above right One of the King's Nympton's oil lamps amongst some trees in 1993. Most were sold in the 1960s for £4 10s 0d each, buyer collects! This included the lamp post itself on condition that the platform surface was made good following uprooting. Station names were etched on to the lamp glass, but plain glass was fitted at King's Nympton at the time of the name change. *TG*

This really *is* the 1960s, unlike the photograph of the engine of the same class at Lapford (page 22). Two Class '4MT' engines, Nos 80039 and 80043, are on a special train from Torrington and Ilfracombe. This was probably the last steam working on the line until 1994 and took place on 12 September 1965. A study of these photographs of King's Nympton (and those elsewhere in this book) shows the gradual reduction in facilities, from two platforms with signal box and passing loop, to a single line, one platform and no staff or booking facilities.

The station buildings have been in private ownership for several years and were put up for sale in 1994. Passengers are provided with a small bus-type waiting shelter. The hotel, which was advertised on the coach house roof, has recently closed. This was the Fortescue Arms and Earl Fortescue, who lived at Weare Giffard (see page 102), had a say in the location of some of the stations on the line. *Ronald Lumber/TG*

These two photographs of Station Road in King's Nympton village were taken about 70 years apart, yet only super-ficial changes have occurred. The shops on either side of the road (a general stores and boot-maker) have become private houses, and the view of the field is hidden by trees that have grown on the site of the building beyond the horses. There is also a school on the right just beyond the bottleneck. 'The Arms' notice hanging over the road may refer to the 'Fortescue Arms' at the bottom of the hill by the station. *Beaford Archive/TG*

Above Just north of King's Nympton the railway crosses the river at Junction Pool, to which reference is made in *Tarka the Otter*. This is the junction of the rivers Taw and Mole, the railway continuing to follow the former. The nearby King's Nympton Park Estate is owned by the Wildfowl Trust. *TG*

Right Between King's Nympton and the next station of Portsmouth Arms there are attractive views from the railway on both sides of the train. Good views of the railway are also plentiful, such as this one showing the 17.24 from Exeter St David's to Barnstaple on 18 August 1989. *TG*

Portsmouth Arms was another station without a village, and was named after the 4th Earl of Portsmouth of Eggesford House, under whose auspices the Exeter Road to Barnstaple was built. At several points on this road the old toll houses can still be seen.

Above Portsmouth Arms station approach, with traditional telephone box and car, seen in the summer of 1986. The platforms are to the right behind the notice board and the main road on the far left. *TG*

Below An evening train (unit No 954) heading toward Exeter on 24 August 1989. The Station Master's house, now in private hands, is in the background. *TG*

An Ilfracombe to Exeter train passes through Portsmouth Arms on a wet spring day in 1968 hauled by Class '42' 'Warship' locomotive No D812 *The Royal Naval Reserve 1859-1959.*

On 30 April 1994 the 08.24 Exmouth to Barnstaple train is the second of the day to stop at the much reduced station, formed of Class '150' No 150244. *Both TG*

Opposite A typical early 1960s train on the 'Tarka Line' is seen at Portsmouth Arms *en route* to Ilfracombe, hauled by 'Battle of Britain' Class No 34072 *257 Squadron*.

By 1966 the loop had been taken out and only the down platform was in use. The 17.45 Exeter Central to Ilfracombe passes through Portsmouth Arms on 28 May 1966. *Lens of Sutton/Ronald Lumber*

Above The present-day station is even more bare, with no signal box or main buildings. The old up platform is overgrown, but at least the station is still open as a request stop. At the time of writing there were three trains to Barnstaple and four in the other direction on weekdays. Modern lighting has replaced the oil lamps, one of which is now in the grounds of the nearby Portsmouth Arms public house. *TG*

London and South Western Ry.
—
787
TO
PORTSMOUTH ARMS

A little beyond Portsmouth Arms station on the Exeter Road is a staggered crossroads with byroads to the east and west. The surfacing of the road, modifications to the houses and growth of trees in the background does not prevent recognition of the present (1993) with the past (turn of the century) photographs. The view is looking towards Portsmouth Arms; the road to the left (out of sight beyond the houses) leads to a bridge over the railway line, from which there are excellent views towards Exeter. *Beaford Archive/TG*

Looking from that bridge on 21 August 1990, we see unit No 879 forming the 16.05 Exeter Central to Barnstaple train. *TG*

38

The adjacent field also gives a good view. On 29 April 1994 the train is worked by a Class '150' Sprinter.

The same location a few days *later* finds a steam train heading for Barnstaple. This is the outward working of the special train shown on page 22; the engine is Standard Class '4MT' No 80079. *Both TG*

Shortly before reaching Umberleigh the train slows down as it passes over a minor road. This is Umberleigh Gates, although the level crossing gates were removed in 1972 and the crossing is now open. On 22 August 1987 Class '33' No 33050 takes the 10.13 fast train (with two intermediate stops) to Exeter.

Much shorter trains are now the norm, represented by this 'Sprinter' working the 10.18 from Barnstaple to Exmouth on 30 April 1994. The crossing is located by the white house on the right. *Both TG*

This view overlooking Umberleigh, with the station in the background, was taken from a nearby hill in the early years of the railway.

The hill is now covered with trees, but a similar viewpoint can be obtained from behind the Rising Sun public house. Most of the buildings can still be recognised, although the station is partly obscured by the premises of Murch Bros, who deal in farming equipment which used to be delivered by rail. Both photographs show the road bridge over the River Taw in the foreground. *Beaford Archive/TG*

The original road bridge over the Taw was of narrow wooden construction and is seen here from the east bank, with the Rising Sun and the Exeter Road in the background.

The bridge was rebuilt during the First World War, but the view over the river has otherwise hardly changed. *Beaford Archive/TG*

Left The stone commemorating the rebuilding. *TG*

The Umberleigh to Barnstaple section of the line formed what was called the Taw Valley Extension and was opened in 1854. Umberleigh is a most attractive station by virtue of the road overbridge at the northern end, the wide arches of which are evidence that the line was originally built to the broad gauge. The line was doubled from here to Barnstaple in 1890. This is the view in 1968.

The signal box was closed in 1971 when the line to Barnstaple was singled, and this 1994 view shows that it has now been demolished. Class '153' No 153302 has just made a brief stop on a late afternoon train from Exeter, from which three passengers alighted. *Both TG*

Opposite and above A pleasant view of the station and the countryside lying to the south is obtained from the road bridge. Class '142' No 142019 pauses on its way to Barnstaple on 22 August 1986. Behind the train can be seen the sign imposing a speed restriction for Umberleigh Gates. In the right foreground is the remains of the short bay for the end loading of vehicles.

One of the locomotive-hauled trains brought in to substitute for a shortage of DMUs following the withdrawal of Class '142' units is seen at the same place in the summer of 1987. The engine is Class '33' No 33050.

One of the latest generation of diesel units, Class '150' No 150244, leaves Umberleigh as the 16.05 from Exeter Central on 30 April 1994. *All TG*

SOUTHERN RAILWAY.

(10/24)

Stock
787

TO

UMBERLEIGH

Right The external views of Umberleigh, Morchard Road and Copplestone stations are very similar - this is Umberleigh in 1994. *TG*

Left In common with the other stations on the line, Umberleigh had a goods yard with road access, guarded by a five-bar gate. The yard is now abandoned, and the gate, serving no useful function, is left permanently open and is gradually being hidden by encroaching natural growth. The Southern Railway recognised the attraction of the area for holiday makers and Umberleigh yard was one of several locations where Camping Coaches were available. *TG*

Below The railway bridge over the River Taw immediately after Umberleigh station can be seen from the road bridge over the river. Here a 'Sprinter' negotiates the bridge on 30 August 1993. *TG*

Contrasts on the line between Umberleigh and Chapelton. A Barnstaple-bound train is seen on 20 April 1992, then at the same location two years *later* is a steam train, which must have been something of a surprise to anyone walking down the path from which this photograph was taken! *Both TG*

Above Distances along the line were traditionally recorded from Waterloo at 1/4-mile intervals. Milepost 207 was immediately prior to reaching Chapelton, the last station before Barnstaple. *TG*

Below The green enamel nameboard at Chapelton was erected in Southern Railway days. The LSWR lamp post to the left has had its lamp removed. *TG*

Top Public access to Chapelton station is along a short unmade road also serving as a public footpath, which crosses the railway and the River Taw. *TG*

Above The comments about the then recently introduced open station system hardly apply at Chapelton. There is no ticket barrier and there are rarely more than two or three intending passengers. *TG*

Past and Present Colour

The Tarka Trail

A line for all seasons - this first pair of photographs does not show change across the years, but just from season to season in this most beautiful part of England. The first shows the 'Tarka Line' in the summer of 1994; Class '150' No 150219 is seen near Portsmouth Arms on a Barnstaple-bound train.

The same location in winter is in some ways more attractive and gives an indication of the beauty to be seen outside the holiday season. Class '153' No 153382 is heading for Exeter. *Terry Gough/Stuart Smallridge*

An up train approaches King's Nympton on 28 July 1963. This is the 09.55 Ilfracombe to Waterloo service hauled by 'Battle of Britain' Class No 34072 *257 Squadron*. The wooden signal guarding the down line is a survivor of the LSWR; by this time almost all others had been replaced by iron lattice or rail-built posts with metal arms. The bridge in the background carries the Exeter Road to Barnstaple.

September 1994 finds both the railway and the road downgraded. The 'Tarka Line' is now a branch rather than a main line and the Exeter Road has lost its importance following the building of the North Devon Link Road from the M5 motorway to Barnstaple. The train is the 10.10 from Barnstaple to Exmouth consisting of Class '150' No 150238. *Lawrence Golden/Terry Gough*

Barnstaple Junction during the diesel locomotive era finds Class '22' No D6313 outside the goods shed on 8 June 1967. The main station buildings are beyond the shed and the island platform is to the left, just out of view.

The present-day trains seem dwarfed by the platform built to accommodate the long London-bound services. The goods yard has been cleared and the view of the houses in the background is partly obscured by new buildings. The goods shed is isolated from the railway and has taken on a distinct lean to the right. *Frank Hornby/Terry Gough*

Barnstaple Town station long after the last train had departed. It was expected that the station would be demolished as the track and signalling had already been removed. The building itself was clearly in a poor state of repair.

However, the area subsequently sprang to life. The present view, while very different, clearly shows that a railway once passed here. The station buildings and the signal box have been retained, although surrounded by houses. The station buildings were used as a restaurant until 1994, but are currently unoccupied. *Both Terry Gough*

The long climb out of Ilfracombe gave rise to spectacular sights in the days of heavy steam-hauled trains. On 27 July 1963 'Battle of Britain' Class No 34079 *141 Squadron* pilots Class '4300' No 7333 on an evening train to Taunton.

The embankment along this stretch of line is now overgrown, although the foot and cycle path gives an opportunity to follow the course of the railway. Identifying particular spots is difficult, but the unusual bare tree in the centre background eliminated any doubt when it came to this one. *Lawrence Golden/Terry Gough*

A special train masquerading as the 'Atlantic Coast Express' passes Instow on 2 April 1978 hauled by Class '33' No 33105 on a tour from Waterloo to Meldon and Meeth.

Although Instow is closed there is much evidence of the railway with the restored signal box, most of the station and even some track. This is the same location in September 1994 showing the trackbed in its new guise as the Tarka Trail. *Spencer Taylor/Terry Gough*

Class '25' No 25170 leaves Torrington for Barnstaple with clay from Meeth and Marland clay works in October 1977. The main station platform and building is to the right, although little remains of the platform on the other side.

Cyclists now use the Tarka Trail where trains once passed. The station building is now a public house giving a sound excuse to rest before continuing one's journey. *Spencer Taylor/Terry Gough*

Watergate Halt was in most attractive surroundings and was well worth a visit, whether or not to catch one of the very infrequent trains. This is the halt in June 1967.

Watergate forms part of today's Tarka Trail. Some visitors make a point of cycling along the platform, an activity not permitted at stations still in use! *Frank Hornby/Terry Gough*

Chapelton at the turn of the century, with the traditional line-up of staff for the photographer. The points in the foreground give access to a siding, in later years used to take timber from the adjacent sawmills, which are still in operation although there is no longer a siding here. The public footpath to the river can be seen in the foreground, and also gives access to the platform.

In contrast to the other stations along the 'Tarka Line', when the track was singled it was not the platform with the main building that was retained at Chapelton. The down platform is used, and the station house, which was on the up side, is now a private residence. Only a few trains stop at Chapelton on weekdays. It is, however, in the unique position of having a Sunday service on only one occasion during the year, when all trains stop and there are more passengers than the total for a week. The reason for this activity is that the annual Chapelton steam fair is held nearby and the service is provided to encourage visitors to use the train, a commendable local initiative. One of these Sunday stopping trains pulls away from Chapelton on 27 August 1989 toward Barnstaple. The train is formed of two single-car units (Nos 103 and 105, both of Class '122') and two-coach unit No 955 (Class '108'). *Beaford Archive/TG*

Two miles beyond Chapelton, at New Bridge, the Exeter Road crosses both the river and the railway before reaching the village of Bishop's Tawton. This is the approach to the village on the Exeter Road in the early 1900s, showing the parish church of St John the Baptist and the school immediately in front.

The main road was re-routed many years ago and the cottages are now spared the incessant noise and danger from modern-day through traffic. The main road can be seen at the foot of the hill passing left to right towards Barnstaple. New houses have been built opposite the cottages and the school, which was built in 1841, now serves as the village hall. The road past the cottages forms part of the north-east segment of the Tarka Trail from Barnstaple to Lynton. *Beaford Archive/TG*

For the remaining short journey to Barnstaple the scenery is far less interesting. The railway first crosses the River Taw yet again, then passes under the North Devon Link Road. Immediately thereafter on the right is the embankment of the line that once connected the GWR and LSWR systems; there is now a cycle and footpath along the old line.

The LSWR station of Barnstaple Junction, now referred to as plain Barnstaple, is situated on the western edge of the town, which is a short walk away over the impressive Taw Bridge. Barnstaple Junction was an important railhead, with two long platforms, a large goods yard, two signal boxes and an engine shed. In 1924 one of the platforms was converted into an island, thus increasing the capacity of the station to handle the summer holiday traffic.

However, it must be acknowledged that passenger traffic has fallen drastically since steam days, although the provision of just one coach on some trains, particularly during the summer, is rather extreme and results in severe overcrowding, as seen in the photograph below.

Travelling hopefully, or, perhaps more to the point, hopefully travelling. Intending passengers for the return journey to Exeter await the arrival of single-coach Class '122' unit No 106, forming the 12.45 from Exmouth on 24 July 1992. Overcrowding seems inevitable.
Both TG

This is Barnstaple Junction station in the early years of the Southern Railway, with Class 'X6' No 665 on an Exeter train. This engine was scrapped in 1933.

The 1962 view shows virtually no changes, other than the use of more modern motive power and rolling-stock. 'West Country' Class No 34023 *Blackmore Vale* stands in the same platform with an Ilfracombe to Exeter train on 21 April.

The same place on 16 August 1986. The train is the 16.00 all-stations (except Newton St Cyres) to Exeter hauled by Class '33' No 33211. This was one of only a few members of this class built with narrow bodies especially for the Hastings line, and it is not clear why it was so far from home territory. *Lens of Sutton/Terry Nicholls/TG*

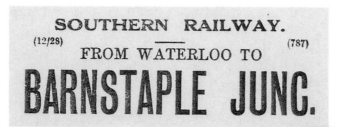

Opposite The last days of long locomotive-hauled trains were imminent when this photograph was taken, a year later almost to the day, in 1987. Class '31' No 31208 arrives on the Saturdays-only 15.48 from Exeter St David's. It was only on summer Saturdays that 1st Class accommodation was provided, and a study of the public timetable thus gave the clue as to which trains were scheduled to be locomotive-hauled and which were diesel multiple units.

What a contrast is this 1993 photograph, showing a two-coach train entering the station. The signal box ('A' box) has been demolished, all sidings have been removed and the centre island platform is falling into disrepair. Class '150' No 150240 arrives as the 14.15 from Exmouth on 30 August 1992. *Both TG*

Above The interior of 'A' box was a good example of a traditional signal box where all operations were undertaken manually. It closed in November 1987, and shortly afterwards all semaphore signals were removed from the whole of the 'Tarka Line'. *TG*

Opposite Views of the station from the nearby road bridge also show that changes have taken place in relatively recent times. Class '42' No D805 *Benbow* has just arrived with the 08.10 from Paddington on 17 July 1971. Track alterations were taking place following closure of the line on to Ilfracombe, although the line in the foreground was still in use for freight trains to Torrington and beyond. Barnstaple's second signal box is just visible on the extreme left.

By 1987 there was no obvious trace of the junction for Ilfracombe, part of the land being taken over by Western Truck Rental. The goods yard had been closed in March and the track was in the process of being ripped up. Further changes have since taken place - there is now only one track and this terminates at the end of the main platform. *Ronald Lumber/TG*

Above right and right There was a bulk cement depot in the yard with a daily delivery. Class '31' No 31403 waits to leave for Exeter Riverside with the empty tanks on 27 August 1986. This service ceased the following year.

The whole area has since been cleared and part is now occupied by retail stores. There are plans for even more rationalisation (ie reduction of facilities), with a new basic station to be built a few yards closer to Exeter. The existing building is most attractive and was refurbished only a few years ago; it would be unfortunate if it was lost in the interests of further development of the site for non-railway purposes. *Both TG*

The shed that housed engines for the heavy passenger and freight trains and the smaller engines for local services fell into disrepair in BR days and was without a roof by the time this photograph was taken. It formally closed in 1971 and was subsequently demolished, hardly a difficult task. *R. C. Riley*

The signalman in Barnstaple West (or 'B') box has just collected the token from the crew of a train from Ilfracombe on 23 April 1962. The engine is 'West Country' Class No 34015 *Exmouth*.

In the second view Class '2MT' 2-6-2T No 41248 shunts the stock of the 14.40 from Torrington, while Type 2 diesel-hydraulic No D6328 waits for the Torrington portion of the 10.15 Waterloo to Ilfracombe train on 27 June 1964.

This was the site of the junction on 22 August 1987. The line to the left now only continued for a few hundred yards beyond the bridge, and after closure of the Torrington line was used to store rolling-stock and for running-round purposes. The locomotive is Class '31' No 31208.

Today the track has all gone, but in its place is the beginning of the Tarka Trail to Bideford and beyond forming the south-west segment of the Trail's 'figure eight'. *Terry Nicholls/Ronald Lumber/TG/TG*

This location is just beyond the junction of the two lines, seen in 1968. In the foreground is the line to Torrington, with access to the junction guarded by an LSWR gantry signal. The line curving away into the distance crosses the River Taw just out of sight before reaching Barnstaple Town station.

The Barnstaple to Ilfracombe line, which was opened in 1874, lasted almost 100 years, being closed by BR in 1970. There were attempts by private organisations to run the line, but these did not come to fruition. Today the embankment has been grassed and the trackbed on the other side of the river to Braunton forms part of the Tarka Trail. *Both TG*

3
THE TARKA TRAIL:
NORTHERN SECTION

The north-east segment of the Tarka Trail across the edge of Exmoor starts from Barnstaple Junction station and, once it leaves the Barnstaple area, is not suitable for cyclists, as it does not use old railways. It does, however, cross two former lines, and to that extent has a place in this book. We shall travel round this section of the 'figure eight' in an anti-clockwise direction, from Barnstaple round via Lynmouth, Lynton, Ilfracombe and Mortehoe, and back to Barnstaple.

Opposite Starting from Barnstaple Junction station, the route crosses the attractive bridge over the River Taw. The railway crossed at the same point, which gave good views of the trains to and from Ilfracombe. A freight train bound for Ilfracombe in the early 1960s is hauled by Class 'N' No 31846. Barnstaple Town station is just beyond the signal box on the east bank.

The railway bridge was dismantled in 1977 and the view from the road bridge looking north is now unimpeded. The skyline has changed and the modern three-storey buildings on the riverside are adjacent to the old Barnstaple Town station, which still exists (see pages 83-4). The much taller building beyond is the Civic Centre, housing the offices of North Devon District Council and Devon & Cornwall Constabulary. *R. C. Riley/TG*

Right These two Knight advertisments date from 1924 and 1994 and are grandfather and grandson. Several of Mr Knight senior's photographs are reproduced in this book, including the one seen here.

Above and right At the town end of the road bridge is the North Devon Museum, and from here the Trail follows the east bank of the river, from which excellent views are obtained of the bridge. The factory of Messrs Shapland on the west bank is evident in both photographs, which were taken about 60 years apart. There is an expanding cycle route network within Barnstaple and apart from encouraging cycling for local journeys, it also serves as a convenient link between the southern and northern sections of the Tarka Trail. *R. L. Knight/TG*

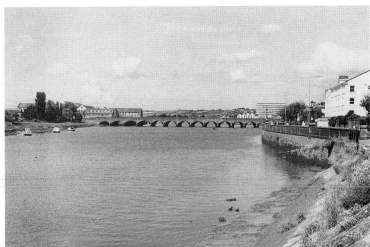

While in this part of Barnstaple, it is worth a short diversion at Newport to visit the site of the GWR's Victoria station and goods yard, much of which is now buried under what is named the Great Western Industrial Estate. One of the railway buildings has, however, survived, and this is the goods shed, part of which is now a Christian church. A main road covers the railway trackbed adjacent to the platform, while the platforms themselves are mostly within a South Western Electricity depot. *R. L. Knight/TG*

The Trail joins the A377 (Exeter Road) after passing under the North Devon Link Road. At Bishop's Tawton (already visited on page 50) the Trail leaves the main road and shortly thereafter becomes a footpath to Landkey. Although there is no railway station at Landkey, the GWR line from Taunton passed close to the village and the main road (Blakes Hill Road) passed through the centre of the village. There is little trace of the railway today; the trackbed lies under the North Devon Link Road, the new A361.

The main road through Landkey in the days before the village was inflicted with the continual passage of motor vehicles. The end cottage was a filling station, and on the extreme right was a general stores. The road leading from the right is Tanners Road.

Thanks to the North Devon Link Road the village has claimed back much of the quiet of former days, as the old main road is now used mostly by local traffic. All the cottages on the right are now private residences. *Beaford Archive/TG*

After leaving the Landkey area, the Trail heads east until it reaches the River Bray; the North Devon Link Road uses the former railway viaduct to cross the river. The Trail then heads north across Exmoor and has no further interaction with railways until it reaches Lynmouth.

My first visit to Lynmouth served as a dramatic demonstration of both the beauty and destructive power of nature. This was the summer of 1952 shortly after the floods that destroyed most of the village and caused considerable loss of life. Here was a peaceful village built at the mouth of the East and West Lyn Rivers surrounded by the steep sides of the valley. With little warning this peace was literally shattered, and the character of the village permanently changed. The visitor today will still encounter beauty in the river and its surroundings, although they now look very different.

Immediately above Lynmouth is Lynton, reached by a cliff railway opened in 1890 and still providing by far the quickest and least exhausting mode of transport between the two villages. The cliff railway was financed by Sir George Newnes and built by Mr R. Jones. These two people played the same roles in relation to Lynton Town Hall (see page 68). The railway consists of two adjacent tracks on each of which is a single coach attached to a common cable. Each coach houses a tank and by filling the coach at the top of the incline with water, it becomes heavier than the one at the bottom and, as it descends, the bottom coach ascends.

The best view of the cliff railway is from the mouth of the river at Lynmouth. All the buildings shown in the early photograph still stand, although the tower (the Rhenish Tower) was destroyed during the 1952 flood and rebuilt two years later. The unusually designed corner building is now a gift shop with holiday accommodation above, while the thatched building is the Rising Sun Hotel. A new wall separating the harbour from the river was built following the flood. *Bill Pryor/TG*

There was another railway here, the Lynton & Barnstaple Railway (L&BR), which was also financed by Sir George Newnes. It was opened in 1898 and provided both passenger and freight facilities until complete closure in 1935.

Above An advertisement for the L&BR. *Courtesy Bill Pryor*

Above The terminus of the line was situated even higher than Lynton village. Much has been written about this railway and it is regrettable that it was closed long before its potential value as a tourist attraction in its own right was recognised.

The station buildings are now in use as a private residence and externally are almost unchanged. The main building includes accommodation to let during the holiday season, and the goods shed has also been converted into residential accommodation. There are other surviving stations on the line, particularly Woody Bay (see page 69) and Blackmoor Gate, but the course of the railway is far from the Tarka Trail. *Bill Pryor/TG*

Above The station nameboard survives at the Exmoor Museum in Lynton. *TG*

London and South Western Ry.

787

TO

LYNTON

Via BARNSTAPLE TOWN.

Lynton has an imposing Town Hall in Lee Road, which is still used for this purpose. The old photograph is obviously pre-1918 as there is no war memorial. There are still shops opposite the Town Hall, currently including an art studio and a printers, the latter selling excellent old photographs of the Lynton & Barnstaple Railway. The printer himself owns the old railway station. *Beaford Archive/TG*

The Trail picks up the North Devon Coast Path through the Valley of the Rocks, past Lee Abbey (now a Christian conference and holiday centre) towards Woody Bay. The Lynton & Barnstaple Railway had a station named Woody Bay at the highest point on the line, but this was almost 2 miles inland at Martinhoe Cross, which is now on the A39 main road. At Woody Bay itself there is the remains of a pier, once part of a plan to develop the Bay as a tourist centre with arrival by steamer being one option and train another.

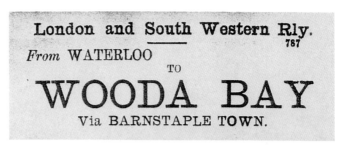

London and South Western Rly.
787
From WATERLOO
TO
WOODA BAY
Via BARNSTAPLE TOWN.

Woody Bay station, which was built by Mr R. Jones, is now privately owned and in most attractive surroundings. Both the hamlet and the station were formerly called Wooda Bay, the name changing in 1901. *Bill Pryor/TG*

Beyond Woody Bay the Coast Path continues to Heddon's Mouth and over Trentishoe and Holdstone Downs to the village of Combe Martin. Most of the area is designated of special scientific interest and is in the care of the National Trust. Continuing west the Coast Path approaches Ilfracombe over Hillsborough, which gives very good views of the harbour and the town beyond.

Ilfracombe railway station was located high above the town near Cairn Top. Many of the trains from London to Barnstaple ran on to Ilfracombe, which was the end of the line. The road seen in this old view of the town leads past the then new entrance to the station on the extreme left and continues round the base of the hill. A zigzag path from here takes one to Cairn Top, which gave an excellent view of the station.

The lorry (top left) is parked on the station approach road, now used for access to a factory built on the station site. The rear gardens of the houses nearest the camera in the 'past' view are now occupied by modern bungalows. The houses beyond the station approach still stand and many continue to offer bed and breakfast accommodation, despite closure of the railway. Houses also occupy the field on the right, where the merry-go-round can be seen. The Cairn is a Nature Reserve administered by Devon Wildlife Trust, and a visit to Cairn Top today finds the view obscured by trees; even in winter it is difficult to see the station site or the town. *Ilfracombe Museum/TG*

The station was rebuilt by the Southern Railway in 1928/9. Here the 'Atlantic Coast Express' waits to leave for Waterloo on 12 July 1957 behind 'Battle of Britain' Class No 34060 *25 Squadron*.

As the number of rail passengers declined, the trains became shorter and were eventually formed of single or two-car diesel multiple units, which were dwarfed beside the long island platform. This is the station in 1968, still open but already looking abandoned. *Frank Hornby/TG*

The Tarka Trail continues to use the North Devon Coast Path from Ilfracombe to Woolacombe, with its famous stretch of sandy beach, then to Croyde Bay and Braunton Burrows, before meeting the railway again. Apart from the section between Woolacombe and Putsborough, the Coast Path is unsuitable for cyclists and an alternative is to take the course of the railway from behind the site of Ilfracombe station, which is a designated cycle and footpath. This takes one almost as far as the next station up the line, namely Mortehoe & Woolacombe. 'Up' is a most appropriate term, as the line climbs at a gradient of 1 in 36 almost all the way and is thus marginally steeper than the line connecting Exeter Central and St David's.

The railway was cut out the side of the hill and passes above the Slade Valley. The road through Slade village leads from Ilfracombe to Mortehoe & Woolacombe station. The cycle track stops at Lee Bridge, a little short of the site of this station, from which point the road can be used to reach Woolacombe village and the Tarka Trail proper. There is also a permissive footpath from Lee Bridge which uses the railway as far as Morte Bridge.

The view from the train in 1957 with Slade village lying to the left. Ilfracombe engine shed and station awning are just visible in the distance. The old railway line forms part of the Nature Reserve and passes through the up line tunnel and past two reservoirs in the valley below. The industrial building and chimney in the present-day view mark the site of Ilfracombe station. *Frank Hornby/TG*

Mortehoe & Woolacombe station in 1968, shortly after the up line had been removed as part of economies, which in the event were insufficient to prevent the line from closing. Morte Bridge is immediately beyond, and adjacent to the station is another 'Fortescue Arms' (see pages 30-1).

Remarkable events began to take place at the station in 1985. The buildings had been in private ownership for some years, but the platforms were abandoned and the track had been taken up. New track and several coaches appeared, as if a long deferred reinstatement of services was about to become a reality. But the reality was that this once country station was to become a children's playground.

This was opened in 1987, with an entrance fee far in excess of the cost of a platform ticket! By 1994, when this photograph was taken, the shallow cutting beyond the station had been filled in and Morte Bridge had been removed as part of a scheme to realign the road junction. The field to the right is used in summer weekends for an open air market and car boot sale - the ultimate desecration of the countryside! *All TG*

London and South Western Ry.

787

TO

MORTEHOE

South of Mortehoe & Woolacombe the railway line descended sharply (1 in 40) all the way to Braunton, following the main Ilfracombe to Barnstaple road (the A361). The railway was built long before this road, and in Victorian times the road between Barnstaple and Ilfracombe was what is now the B3230 through Muddiford, more direct but much hillier.

The station in Braunton was situated where the road to Croyde crossed the railway. In this photograph, taken in the early 1920s and looking toward Ilfracombe, the level crossing can be seen between the two engines. It was here that, in steam days, additional engines were attached to heavy trains to give assistance on the long climb to Mortehoe.

The same location in 1968 shows that there have been no major structural changes to the station buildings, although a house has been built on the Croyde side of the level crossing. The station is electrically lit, but still guarded by traditional semaphore signals and still providing the same basic seating.

The railway site is now occupied by a Countryside Centre, Health Centre, car park and youth club, the latter being housed in the old goods shed. Only this and the station house, which is now a newsagent, remain. The old-style van glimpsed through the bushes may lead one to assume that this too is an old photograph, but modern telephone boxes confirm that this is the present day. *R. L. Knight/TG/TG*

An almost identical view taken from the other platform on 27 July 1968 shows that the down line has been removed and the only function of the signal box is to protect the level crossing. The train, hauled by Class '42' No D817 *Foxhound*, is the 18.20 from Ilfracombe to Exeter St David's.

Very little survives to link these two pictures except the white shops on the left, the end one of which can be glimpsed above the signal box roof in the 'past' view. The level crossing was where the pedestrian crossing is now located, in the centre of the picture. *Ronald Lumber/TG*

The town centre is only a few yards to the east of the station and is at the intersection of the Croyde and Ilfracombe roads. A bus from Ilfracombe passes through the village in the early 1930s.

Although basically unchanged, the motor cars, proliferation of road markings, telegraph poles and general clutter all spoil what was a pleasant location. *R. L. Knight/TG*

The Tarka Trail approaches Braunton by way of Braunton Burrows, which is a National Nature Reserve, then along the west bank of the River Caen to join the railway line at what was the level crossing at Velator, about half a mile south of Braunton station. From here the Trail uses the railway trackbed all the way to Barnstaple. The only station on this section is Wrafton.

Southern Railway.

5/23   787

TO

WRAFTON

Wrafton station looking towards Ilfracombe, taken during singling of the line in 1967.

The station buildings are now in use as a private house and several railway items have been retained, including the nameboard, platform electric lights and one of the signals (left). *Both TG*

The village of Wrafton is close by and this is the Post Office and general stores on the Barnstaple to Ilfracombe road in the 1920s.

A new main road was later built between this part of the village and the station, and the old route is now only a local road serving recently built houses. The Post Office still exists, however, even to the letter box in the wall.
R. L. Knight/TG

The old Chivenor Airfield, looking across the River Taw towards Barnstaple.
Today Chivenor is also used by the RAF Search and Rescue Helicopter Unit, which was established in 1958. This 1994 photograph was taken from the Tarka Trail. *R. L. Knight/TG*

Shortly after passing Wrafton railway station is Chivenor Royal Air Force Station. An airfield was established here in 1934 to provide passenger and postal services to Lundy Island, South Wales and the South West. The airfield was taken over by the RAF at the beginning of the Second World War and has been used as a fighter pilot training base ever since (except between 1974 and 1980 when it was closed). It is scheduled to close permanently in the near future.

From Chivenor to Barnstaple the railway, today the Tarka Trail, keeps to the north bank of the River Taw and gives good views of the opposite bank including Fremington Quay (see page 88). The Trail passes Heanton Court, which is now a restaurant; the next point of interest is a lime kiln, which was restored in 1986 after falling into disuse at the beginning of the century.

The approach to Barnstaple is past the Pottington Industrial Estate. The Trail leaves the railway once it reaches the site of Pottington level crossing by the grounds of the Rugby Football Club. The railway crossed the River Yeo by a swing bridge which gave access to Rolle Quay and Pilton Wharf, but the bridge has been demolished, requiring a detour round the Quay itself. It is nevertheless worth continuing along the railway to the point where the swing bridge was situated, before retracing one's steps to Pottington level crossing to take up the Trail.

The Trail runs alongside Rolle Quay, crosses the Rolle Bridge (the A361 Ilfracombe road), then along the south bank of the river to regain the railway between the Civic Centre and Barnstaple Town station.

The Town station was built on this site in 1898 (see page 84) and had a platform for the Barnstaple Junction and Ilfracombe trains and a bay from which the Lynton & Barnstaple Railway narrow-gauge trains began their journey.

Even in 1968 the site of the bay for Lynton was readily discernable. The diesel multiple unit is working the 17.18 Exeter Central to Ilfracombe service on 27 July. The iron railway bridge and road bridge behind can be seen in the right background, while the town centre and cattle market lie to the left behind the houses. The modern library and North Devon Record Office are also nearby. The signal box at the far end of the station is now the museum and shop of the Lynton & Barnstaple Railway Association, one of the main aims of which is to rebuild a section of the line, and much railway material has been collected in pursuit of this. Other views of this location are included in the colour photographs. *Bill Pryor/Ronald Lumber*

The station nameboard is still displayed a quarter of a century after closure. *TG*

SOUTHERN
BARNSTAPLE TOWN STATION

A few yards beyond the signal box is the site of the earlier LSWR Town station, on which a bus station was built in 1922. Railway signals can be seen behind the bus station building in this view from the mid-1920s.

This location, The Strand, is readily recognisable today and is still the bus station. The intervening period saw the growth of bus transport, and services were provided by larger and larger double-deck buses wherever they were not precluded by the narrow country roads. The last decade has, however, seen a shrinkage in the use of buses, and almost all services are currently operated by one-man minibuses. Although the cafe in the foreground is now a discotheque, the building still appears to have the same cast iron drainpipes as those seen in the 'past' photograph. Note the contrasting lamp posts in the present-day photograph. *R. L. Knight/TG*

The Strand brings the traveller to the museum by the Taw Bridge, and, by crossing the bridge, back to Barnstaple Junction Station.

4
THE TARKA TRAIL:
SOUTH-WESTERN SECTION

The line from Barnstaple to Fremington was opened in 1848 and wagons were horse-drawn. It was converted to broad gauge in 1854 to connect with the new line from Crediton. It subsequently became part of the LSWR line through to Torrington, following the south bank of the River Taw to Instow where the Taw and Torridge flow into Bideford Bay. This part of the Trail is almost completely flat, but the cyclist in particular should not be lulled into thinking that the ride in one direction will be as easy on the return - the wind can be very strong along this section.

There are several items of railway interest along this stretch of line, for example the remains of a concrete platelayers' hut, one of many hundreds of similar structures used all over the Southern system and made at the concrete works at Exmouth Junction. *TG*

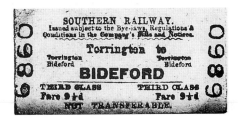

The approach to the first station of Fremington is through a shallow cutting, which opens out to reveal what was once a quay. This was built by the Taw Vale Railway & Dock Company and was used to import coal and export clay from the area around Petersmarland, south of Bideford. This is the station in 1967 when the line and quay were both operational.

The quay ceased to be used for rail-borne traffic in 1970 and subsequently fell into disuse. Likewise the station, which was eventually demolished, and left in the state shown here until the area was prepared for the Tarka Trail. Adjacent to the station was an abattoir built in the 1950s, since closed and demolished in the early 1990s. *Both TG*

In the closing years of steam operation most trains on the Torrington line were operated by BR Standard tank engines of Class '2MT', such as No 41298 seen here. The train is signalled to leave as the 17.46 service from Torrington to Barnstaple Junction on 10 April 1956. Access to the station was from a long railway-owned road from the main A39 road through the village. The main road is now used primarily by local traffic between Barnstaple and Bideford, a new A39, an extension of the North Devon Link Road, having been built between the two towns. The station road is in a poor state of repair and is now all but impassable for cars after heavy rain. *TG*

London and South Western Ry.
———
787
TO
Fremington

The railway next crosses a small creek known as the Pill, and from here a good overall view of the quayside and the adjacent station and sidings could be obtained. The iron bridge was built in 1880 to replace a wooden swing bridge.

   The same view today shows the popularity of the Trail. The footpath to the right leads to Fremington village and the Tarka Trail continues along the trackbed of the railway. *R. L. Knight/TG*

The line continues west and runs perfectly straight until it reaches East Yelland. There was no railway station here, but in the 1950s, amidst much local controversy, a power station complete with a jetty for deliveries of coal was built between the railway and the river bank. Sidings were included and brought some revenue to the railway. It was officially opened on 21 April 1955 by Earl Fortescue, but had a life of less than 40 years before being decommissioned in 1984. There followed more controversy over its fate, and it was eventually demolished.

The land is now derelict and inaccessible due to contamination, and yet again there is argument over whether a housing development should be allowed to proceed. The only building remaining is the one on the far left of the 'past' photograph, seen here from a slightly different angle. This is one of the least attractive sights along the Tarka Trail, and is a demonstration of man's insensitivity. There is a footpath round the perimeter of the power station site that passes the jetty, and this can be used as an alternative to the railway line. *Cyril Found/TG*

River and railway line turn south-west for the approach to Instow. After passing the Royal Marines Amphibious Trials and Training Unit, the railway ran behind the village in a shallow cutting. This is the 13.00 from Waterloo to Torrington on 30 June 1958. The Class 'M7' tank engine, No 30252, was attached at Barnstaple, the greater part of the train continuing to Ilfracombe behind a more substantial engine. The same location today shows an unusually deserted Tarka Trail. *Both TG*

On the opposite bank of the River Torridge is Appledore, and a ferry operates between there and Instow. The jetty at Instow is a good place from which to see the row of houses and shops at the south end of the village. In the distance is the railway level crossing, signal box and station, seen in the 1920s.

This almost identical photograph may give rise to confusion. The signal box still stands, suggesting that the railway is still in operation, yet the fare on the ferry is in decimal currency. The photograph was in fact taken in 1993, and Instow signal box, which is a Grade II listed building, has been preserved as a reminder of the former presence of the railway. It is open to visitors on Sundays during the summer, under the care of the Bideford & Instow Railway Group. *R. L. Knight/TG*

Instow station was on a curve, with the main building on the river side. This is the view looking toward Barnstaple in 1967.

In addition to the signal box, the Torrington-bound platform still exists in a good state of repair, together with traditional railway-style railings. On the left are the premises of the North Devon Yacht Club, which owns the main station building, little changed from railway days apart from the loss of the awning. *Both TG*

Right In BR days the station was electrically lit using lamps of an unusual design attached to the old LSWR cast iron posts. *TG*

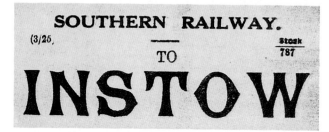

The 17.46 Torrington to Barnstaple Junction train approaches Instow on 30 June 1958 hauled by Class '2MT' No 41298. At the same location over 30 years later, preparations are under way for the Tarka Trail. *Both TG*

Top and above Departure from Instow on 30 June 1958 finds Class 'M7' No 30254 hauling a set of Southern Railway main-line coaches. The train had left Exeter at 16.21 and was due to arrive at Torrington at 18.24. Today yachts dominate the scene; the Tarka Trail runs immediately behind the yachts on the right. *Both TG*

Above right The most attractive front cover of the North Devon Public Transport Guide for the summer of 1993 shows both bus and train at Instow. *Reproduced courtesy of Devon County Council, Environment Department*

Left Another railway item cast in concrete was the gradient post. This one would seem superfluous, as a gradient of 1 in 1000 or 1 in 1155 is hardly significant even for a bicycle, let alone a steam engine. *TG*

When the railway was first built, the terminus for Bideford was at Cross Parks. This later became the goods yard and the railway itself was extended to Torrington in 1872 with a new Bideford station on an embankment above the eastern end of the road bridge over the River Torridge. In this early view, probably dating from the 1930s, the town of Bideford lies across the river.

The goods yard was closed in 1965 and the land is now occupied by private houses built about 10 years ago. The area lay derelict for many years and some of the old quayside buildings towards the bridge still stand. The premises of I. Baker & Son (General Building Material and Coal Merchants) can be seen from Bideford station. *R. L. Knight/TG*

The new station was built in a cramped position and was flanked on one side by the Royal Hotel and on the other by a row of houses in Springfield Terrace. The road approach was under a low bridge then immediately up a steep hill on a sharp bend. This is the view looking toward Barnstaple in 1951 with Class 'M7' No 30255 on a Torrington train.

In common with the other lines on the Tarka Trail, the loop was later taken out as an economy measure, as seen in the second view, dating from the late 1970s. The remaining track was lifted in 1984.

All that was said above about the approach to the station still applies today. The main buildings and platforms still stand and are in excellent repair. A signal box has been reconstructed on the platform, and there is track through the station with signals at each end and a coach in the platform.

The restoration of the station is mainly the work of the Bideford & Instow Railway Group with support from the local authority and numerous other bodies. The Group was formed in 1988 to recreate as far as possible the railway atmosphere at Bideford and Instow railway stations, and this they have already achieved, although no doubt a lot more will be done in the future. The signal box houses the Group's museum which is open to the public on Sunday afternoons from Easter to October. The main station building is owned by Devon County Council and the coach (BR Mark I No 4489, delivered in 1992 from the Mid Hants Railway) is used by the Devon Countryside Service for a natural history display and tea room.

It is most unfortunate that the plans to keep the line open with funding from the European Commission did not materialise. But then perhaps there would have been no new road bridge over the River Torridge and no Tarka Trail, both of which are generally regarded as positive developments. *Lens of Sutton/Alan Wilkinson/TG*

Above A typical station scene from the 1920s, before the advent of milk tank wagons in the 1940s - except that this photograph was taken at Bideford in 1993. *TG*

Below Somewhat older notices can also be inspected, such as this warning about the dangers of nakedness. *TG*

Below right Bideford station is 220½ miles from Waterloo, as indicated on this old plate, which can still be seen by the side of the Tarka Trail. *TG*

Southern Railway.

7/23   TO   787

BIDEFORD

L. & S.W.R.
NEITHER MATCHES
NOR LIGHTS MUST
BE TAKEN NEAR
STORED PARAFFIN

220½ MILES
FROM WATERLOO
STATION LONDON.

There was another railway at Bideford, and this was the Bideford, Westward Ho! & Appledore Railway (BWH&AR), which ran from the town quay to the other places in its title. It was opened in 1901 and ran along the road parallel to the quay, seen here, to Victoria Park where it turned west toward Westward Ho!. It was only 7 miles long and had 13 stations and halts. The railway closed in 1917 and the stock was requisitioned by the Government.

Since the 'past' photograph was taken, the Quay House has acquired a dome and other modifications, the trees have matured and all the attributes of modern society, such as the car park and road markings, are apparent. There is a booking office on the quay from where tickets for Lundy Island can be purchased. *Beaford Archive/TG*

The most attractive (and hilly) part of the Trail accessible to cyclists begins at Bideford, and for those visitors short of time, this is the section for which to aim.

The first major landmark beyond Bideford is an iron bridge that takes the railway over the River Torridge near Landcross. On 22 March 1982 Class '31' No 31286 hauls a train of wagons containing ball clay from Marland to Barnstaple.

The view is easy to locate today, as it is from the main Torrington to Bideford (A386) road. It is fortunate that this and the other bridges over the Torridge were not demolished following closure of the line, as all are now used for the Tarka Trail. Cyclists are visible on the bridge in this 1994 view. Beyond Landcross the railway used part of the old canal route. *David Mitchell/TG*

Road and railway continue to run parallel until the outskirts of Torrington, at times climbing steeply. After passing through a short tunnel under the main road, Weare Giffard can be seen on the opposite bank, a picturesque village most of which straddles a minor road also leading to Torrington.

This old photograph taken adjacent to the railway line shows the village school and quayside cottages. Weare Giffard is the ancestral home of the Fortescue family (see page 31).
   Those buildings can now only be seen from the Tarka Trail during winter, as trees on the embankment block the view. Glimpses of the village can also be had at river level, and this is all that was visible in the spring of 1994, with the old school house still standing. *Beaford Archive/TG*

A short distance further on the railway crosses the river again; a parallel bridge, from where these photographs were taken, carried the Rolle Canal over the River Torridge. It was near here that Tarka the Otter was born and where he was last seen in a fight to the death with a hound. The canal, built by Lord Rolle in 1823, connected the Town Mills with the navigable part of the River Torridge between Weare Giffard and Landcross. It closed in 1871 and the aqueduct is now used to carry a private road into Beam House Activity Centre. On 25 June 1978 Class '33' No 33103 crosses the river with a special passenger train to Torrington. Cyclists and walkers occupy the same position in the 1994 view. *David Mitchell/TG*

The final approach to Torrington station is level, and this close-up view in 1956 shows Class 'M7' No 30247 with through coaches to Waterloo that will form the 'Atlantic Coast Express'.

The same place in 1994 is unrecognisable - the platform is completely overgrown, with the station buildings and road bridge only just visible. But this is deceptive, as the Tarka Trail passes through the station between the original building and the new structure on the left. *Both TG*

London and South Western Ry.
787
TO

TORRINGTON

Right Torrington was one of the few stations in the area privileged to have electric light, which was installed by the Southern Railway. A careful search of the station area today finds that some of the posts still stand. *TG*

Rail-level views from the other end of the platform are clearer. On 23 April 1963 Class '2MT' No 41297 is ready to take just one coach on to Halwill Junction. The main-line coaches on the left are bound for Waterloo.

The same location after the cessation of passenger services shows the station building to be still in good repair, as if waiting to take on another role. Milk trains continued to run from here until 1978, and fertiliser was brought by rail until 1980. The last train from Torrington was a special passenger train, which ran in January 1983. *Terry Nicholls/TG*

A high level view from the road bridge, with plenty of milk traffic in evidence. Class '25' No 25058 undertakes some shunting on 3 September 1978.

The view today is little different, in that the main building still stands and has indeed taken on a new role. It is in everyday use as a public house (The Puffing Billy), which provides refreshment of very good value to the many walkers and cyclists on the Tarka Trail. Little did those responsible for the decision to convert the station into a pub realise that one day customers would arrive by 'rail' again. *Spencer Taylor/TG*

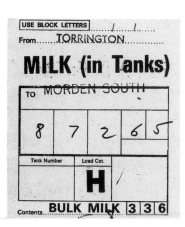

USE BLOCK LETTERS ....../...../.....
From...... TORRINGTON ....

MILK (in Tanks)

TO MORDEN SOUTH

8	7	2	6	5

Tank Number	Load Cat.
	H /

Contents **BULK MILK** | 3 | 3 | 6 |

Rail passengers arriving at Torrington were faced with a long uphill walk to the town, unless they took the bus or one of the taxis that met all major trains. This Victorian era photograph from the hill shows the station in the middle distance and the line stretching toward Barnstaple. In the left foreground is the wooden bridge carrying the narrow-gauge mineral line, which was opened in 1881, to the Marland ball clay works. Clay was transferred to standard-gauge wagons at Torrington and taken to Bideford or Fremington for shipping, or continued by rail to various destinations in mainland Britain.

The view from this location today is rather different, as the road is no longer visible and there are many more trees. The roof of the station, the cottages to the right and the trackbed confirm that this is the same spot. *Beaford Archive/TG*

The nearest village to Torrington station was Taddiport, and this turn-of-the-century photograph shows the village, looking north-east. This was at one time the only route by road to Hatherleigh and Okehampton, but the main road now runs through Torrington town and crosses the River Torridge at Town Mills near the Great Torrington (miniature) Steam Railway and the Royal Horticultural Society's Rosemoor Gardens; it was at Town Mills that several otter hunts used to gather. The mineral line lay some distance behind the camera, having swung west to follow the valley of a tributary of the River Torridge. The Torridge itself is in the foreground.

The cottages still exist today and the village is little changed. A major contributor to the economy of the village, and indeed the surrounding area, was the dairy factory, which opened in 1874. This also provided regular traffic for the railway, particularly milk for the Home Counties. In later years the milk traffic was all transferred to road, and the factory ultimately became a creamery under Dairy Crest, but this was closed in 1993. *Beaford Archive/TG*

Torrington town is located on some of the highest ground in the area and is well worth a visit. There are excellent views of the surrounding countryside and numerous walks over Torrington Common. Part of the Rolle Canal is a footpath. Fortunately the decline of the local dairy industry has to some extent been compensated by the building in 1967 of a glass factory, where the world famous Dartington Crystal is produced.

This is an early photograph of the main road (New Street) through Torrington looking towards Bideford, with the Royal Exchange on the right. The road has been upgraded to form the A386 to Hatherleigh and Okehampton.
Beaford Archive/TG

The narrow-gauge mineral line was replaced in 1925 by a standard-gauge line connected directly to the existing terminus at Torrington. The location of the old mineral railway is clearly indicated at Torrington station, as there is a small arch under the road bridge adjacent to the standard-gauge arch used by the Trail. The new line, known as the North Devon & Cornwall Junction Light Railway, was worked by the Southern Railway from the outset and provided passenger as well as freight services. At its other end it connected with the ex-LSWR North Cornwall line at Halwill Junction, by that time also part of the Southern Railway network.

The bridge carrying the mineral railway was a major landmark that could be seen from the hill between Torrington town and station. The same viewpoint today shows the standard-gauge railway bridge in its new guise as part of the Tarka Trail. *Beaford Archive/TG*

This vantage point gives superb views across the bridge. A mixed passenger and freight train approaches Torrington from Halwill Junction on 27 September 1962 behind Class '2MT' No 41238.

The high bank is now overgrown, but the view from trackbed level is still attractive and opens out dramatically as one approaches the bridge. The line begins to climb just beyond the bridge and becomes increasingly steep over the next 4 miles.

A wider perspective (*right*) shows Class '31' No 31286 approaching Torrington on 22 March 1982 with a ball clay train from Marland. It was only 6 months later that the last clay train ran. *R. C. Riley/TG/David Mitchell*

The new line followed the course of the narrow-gauge line for the first 6 miles. It was built to basic standards and provided several halts in isolated locations, the first of which beyond Torrington was Watergate, seen here in Southern Railway days. The locomotive is Class 'E1/R' No 2095. These engines were rebuilt by the Southern Railway from London, Brighton & South Coast Railway Class 'E1' engines especially for working this line. One coach was normal, as patronage was very poor throughout the lifetime of the line, although both 1st and 3rd Class accommodation was available. From 1964 steam was replaced by a single-coach diesel unit.

The thick foliage behind the platform precludes an identical view, although both 'past' and 'present' photographs are taken from the Torrington end of the platform looking towards the crossing. Many more people pass the halt today than was the case when the trains ran, but this autumn 1994 view in dull weather shows the Trail unusually deserted. *Lens of Sutton/TG*

The railway crosses an ungated road immediately beyond the halt and on 6 October 1978 Class '25' No 25225 approaches the crossing with a train from Meeth and Marland clay works.

Today there are gates protecting users of the trackbed from the road, and preventing motorists from trying to drive along the Trail! *David Mitchell/TG*

The railway continues to climb almost until Yarde Halt is reached, the steepest part being 1 in 45. Yarde served adjacent clay workers' cottages and here also the railway was intersected by a minor road. Long before the advent of the railway, this was the main road from Taddiport to Hatherleigh, and did not lose this status until construction of a new road (now the A386) between the Gribble Inn and Friars Hele. The Gribble Inn, only a mile from Yarde, has recently reopened after a prolonged closure and serves excellent food and drink.

The cottages and platform are still there and on the opposite side of the road is a small car park for those wishing to leave their vehicles and take the Trail. *R. C. Riley/TG*

Lamp posts were normally made of cast iron, but at Watergate and Yarde almost every item of railway furniture was made of concrete, including the lamp posts. All other stations were built of local stone, reflecting the fact that these two halts were not built until the year following the opening of the line. *TG*

117

The line descends steeply to Dunsbear Halt, and thereafter gradients are a little more gentle. Dunsbear Halt was used by men employed at the nearby works of the North Devon Clay Company, and this view, taken in September 1956, shows a mixed train bound for Torrington.

The remnants of the platform are still visible, as is the course of the line. The foreground was once occupied by a short siding. *H. C. Casserley/TG*

Following withdrawal of passenger services between Torrington and Halwill Junction in 1965, the buildings at Dunsbear deteriorated. This is the halt looking towards Halwill in 1967. The siding connecting the 'main' line with the works of the North Devon Clay Company was a few yards south of the halt.

Today the site of the halt is used as a resting place for walkers and cyclists, although self-sufficiency in refreshments is essential. *Both TG*

The entrance to the clay works on 10 February 1981 finds Ruston 0-4-0 diesel shunter 'LEC' and, in the background, Class '31' No 31257. The Halwill line is in the foreground.

The junction of the two lines is now completely obliterated and the only clue to its location is a concrete gate post in the hedgerow, just before the two walkers in the photograph taken in 1993. *Spencer Taylor/TG*

The sidings within the works were extensive and this early view shows the effective use of mechanisation, albeit rather crude. The works' narrow-gauge railway ceased to operate in 1970, and by contrast the present-day view shows the modern automated plant. *Beaford Archive/TG*

Petrockstowe was a more substantial station with a passing loop and two platforms. There was an early morning train from Torrington that ran only as far as here, returning to Torrington after a pause of nearly an hour. There was also a late afternoon train that started from Petrockstowe, but there was no balancing public service bringing the train from Torrington. Timings were very generous at all halts and stations to allow for shunting if the train was mixed. Torrington to Halwill Junction was 20$\frac{1}{2}$ miles, and the scheduled journey time was 1$\frac{1}{2}$ hours. In the first view, taken in the late 1950s, the afternoon Torrington train whittles away the time at Petrockstowe.

The same location in 1982, but a much more overgrown station, finds Class '31' No 31424 travelling from Meeth with a weed-killing train, heading toward Barnstaple on 2 May. Since the line from Meeth to Barnstaple was completely closed a few months later, this seems to have been a pointless exercise.

Today both platforms still exist, but all railway buildings except a platelayers' hut have gone. *Chris Gammell/Spencer Taylor/TG*

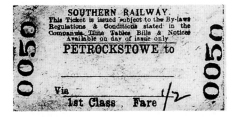

Above Both Instow and Torrington were still issuing Southern Railway tickets to local destinations in the 1960s. Petrockstowe even sold a 1st Class single on 29 July 1963 for 1s 2d, but the booking clerk, probably amazed that anyone should wish to travel 1st Class on an almost empty single-coach branch-line train, forgot to enter the destination. The spelling of Petrockstowe varied during the lifetime of the line, and some tickets omitted the last letter.

Right The Tarka Trail divides here, with cyclists being directed on to a minor road. Walkers can continue along the trackbed almost until the old sidings of the Meeth Clay Company. *TG*

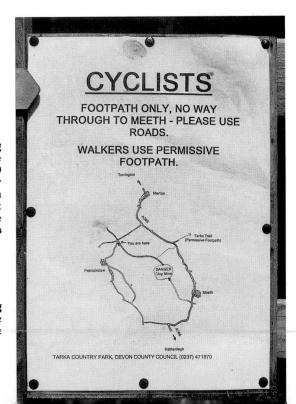

Class '2MT' No 41313 arrives from Torrington in the early 1960s. Today the road still crosses the railway, providing the alternative route of the Trail for cyclists. *Lens of Sutton/TG*

The village of Petrockstowe is about a mile away and it is obvious from its size that the railway could never have realistically expected to have generated much passenger revenue. This is the main street in the 1900s and little is different today, except that the shop has become a private house and telegraph and electric cables intrude. This was the Taddiport to Hatherleigh road; after the building of the new road through Meeth (see page 116), Petrockstowe ceased to be a port of call for through traffic. *Beaford Archive/TG*

About 2 miles south of Petrockstowe station the footpath also leaves the railway line and turns east over fields to join the cycle route at the main road (A386). However, it is possible to continue along the trackbed beyond this point for a few hundred yards to reach the site of the sidings of the Meeth Clay Company. A few loaded wagons are seen here in the 1920s, awaiting collection by the next train.

This is the same location today. The path stops here, as both in front and to the right is the extensive quarrying operation of what is now part of the ECC Group of Companies. The narrow-gauge railway within the clay works closed in 1969. *Beaford Archive/TG*

Meeth Halt was 1 mile beyond the works by train and was the only place where the line crossed a main road (A386); most of the trackbed on this section is now a road leading to the works from the A386. A few years ago there was a clear view of the road from the Torrington end of the platform, and despite having been closed for two years when this visit was made in 1967, no one had seen fit to remove the station nameboard. Beyond Meeth the line closed completely when passenger services between Torrington and Halwill Junction were withdrawn in 1965, and the track was lifted the following year.

The halt is still in existence although nature is gradually embracing both platform and waiting hut. *Both TG*

The village of Meeth is close by and these two photographs taken about 70 years apart show remarkably little change - the cottage has been extended and this is now the Post Office. The Tarka Trail itself does not pass through Meeth, but the detour of about 2 miles is worth the effort, both to visit the station site and to call at the Bull & Dragon public house (to the right of the photograph) where excellent food is served. *Beaford Archive/TG*

The Trail regains the main (A386) road at the small market town of Hatherleigh, and follows the main road through the town before taking the road to the right (South Street), which is signposted to Monkokehampton and Winkleigh.

This is Bridge Street, Hatherleigh (the main road), in the 1920s looking toward Torrington. Locating this point proved quite difficult in 1994, as the road junction has been changed and the corner shop of Messrs Beaven was demolished in the 1960s to reveal the thatched cottages behind. The bakery advertising Hovis still stands, however, and this was the first clue, although it is now a private house. Some of the cottages on the left have been demolished and a new Town Hall built. On the left the steep-gabled building confirms the location. *Beaford Archive/TG*

Above This pre-nationalisation photograph shows the Torrington train worked by Class 'E1/R' No 2095; these were the norm until the BR Standard engines were introduced in 1953. Hatherleigh station was inconveniently situated north-west of the town; reaching it involved first a steep climb along the main road, then a long descent down a country lane. Both the town and the station are on the River Lew which flows into the Torridge just north of the station.

Below A view of the other end of the station in the early 1960s, with Class '2MT' No 41298 on a ball clay train for Halwill Junction. By this time the wooden post signals had been replaced by rail-built posts. *Both Lens of Sutton*

(7/89) SOUTHERN RAILWAY.

(787)

FROM WATERLOO TO

HATHERLEIGH

A close-up view of the Halwill end of the station during a visit two years after closure found most of the ironmongery still in place. The bridge in the background brings the country lane from Hatherleigh past the station approach road (see overleaf). The signals and water crane are those seen in the lower photograph opposite. *TG*

131

This photograph, taken from almost under the lane bridge seen in the picture on the previous page, shows the approach road and was taken shortly after the line was opened and before the installation of water cranes.

Today the cutting between the station and bridge is completely overgrown, but the approach road is clear and forms the private access road to the former station buildings, which have been extended and are now a private residence. *Beaford Archive/TG*

The railway turns west beyond Hatherleigh to reach Halwill Junction 7¾ miles away; there is a footpath and cycleway using in part the old railway, but this is not the Tarka Trail. The Trail proper turns south-east and, using footpaths and country lanes, passes through Jacobstowe before reaching Okehampton. Between these two places the Trail runs parallel to the River Okement. The main (A386) road between Hatherleigh and Okehampton follows almost exactly the route of the original road through Folly Gate.

Okehampton is well known for a number of reasons: to motorists it was one of the worst bottlenecks on the journey to Cornwall from the Home Counties, as the A30 trunk road passed through the centre of the town. Okehampton is also on the edge of Dartmoor, whose less attractive attributes are a military training area and Meldon Quarry, the latter providing ballast for the railways since its opening in 1897. The quarry and the railway line to Coleford Junction (see page 20) were bought by the ECC Group of Companies in 1994.

Okehampton town centre is dominated by the church, and this is the main road (Fore Street) long before the days of the motor car and its upgrading to form part of the A30.

All the buildings still exist today, although most are now put to different uses. The virtual absence of traffic demonstrates that the photograph was taken after the opening of the Okehampton bypass in 1988. This location is at the intersection of the main road with the road from Hatherleigh to the left, and that to Okehampton station and the moor to the right. The station is high above the town and the railway line clings to the edge of Dartmoor from here to Tavistock.
Beaford Archive/TG

Opposite Okehampton was the interchange point for the Plymouth and North Cornwall lines, the latter via Halwill Junction. It was very busy with both passenger and freight traffic, and even had its own small engine shed, just visible beyond the train on the left. 'West Country' Class No 34106 *Lydford* heads the 13.00 Waterloo to Plymouth train, while Class 'T9' No 30313 waits for connecting passengers before leaving with the 17.51 all-stations service to Halwill Junction and Wadebridge on 11 August 1960. The London train had split at Exeter Central, the rear portion being for Ilfracombe, where it was due to arrive at 19.02.

A diesel multiple unit service was operated from Exeter to Okehampton from 1968 to 1972, but all passenger services beyond Okehampton were withdrawn in the former year, except those between Bere Alston and Plymouth. This line still enjoys a service, which continues to Gunnislake on the Cornish side of the River Tamar.

The present-day visitor to the station might think at first glance that there is still a passenger service. The second photograph was taken in 1993 and little seems to have changed. However, the station is in a state of disrepair, the footbridge is unsafe and the platform edges are crumbling. The main buildings are used by several small businesses, the signal box by British Rail maintenance staff, and the track by the ballast trains from Meldon Quarry, 2 miles away. *Both TG*

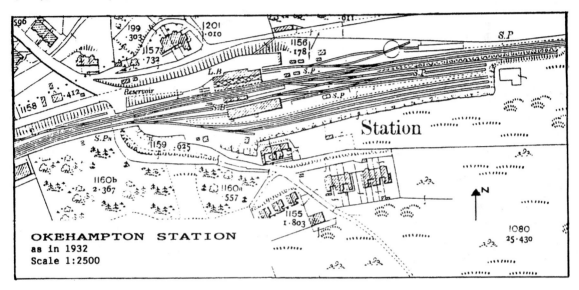

Plan of Okehampton station in 1932. *Courtesy Okehampton Museum of Dartmoor Life*

135

The present station was built by the Southern Railway, and the first photograph (*above left*) shows the original LSWR station. Note that the footbridge was not replaced during the rebuilding, but the new signal box is in a different place from the original.

Even after withdrawal of regular passenger services from Exeter in 1972, Okehampton saw occasional passenger trains, bringing walkers and other visitors. The extremely rare event of Class '142' railbuses in the station was recorded on 23 August 1986; the units are Nos 142019 and 142026.

Okehampton is still worth a visit to see the Meldon trains, although plenty of time and patience are needed. They rarely run to time and are often very early, very late or are cancelled. Here (*above*) two Class '33s', Nos 33039 and 33064, pass through the station on their way to Exeter Riverside on 17 August 1988. *Beaford Archive/TG/TG*

Right In the summer of 1986 there were two passenger trains on each of several Saturdays. These trains were poorly patronised and no similar trains have since been run, although the possibility of reintroducing a regular passenger service from Exeter was under consideration in 1994. *TG*

Above The building of the Okehampton bypass has given new opportunities to see the railway in the vicinity of Okehampton. On 14 August 1991 two Class '33s', Nos 33002 and 33208, descend from Meldon Quarry toward Okehampton. The bypass can be seen in the left background. *TG*

Below Another vantage point is immediately to the west of the station, where the Surbiton 'Motorail' trains once terminated. This was one of the first motorail services in the country and was designed to relieve the worst of the several major hold-ups on the way to the West Country, such as Honiton and Okehampton itself. It ran from 1960 until 1964, but long before it was introduced the site had been used by military trains. On 14 August 1991 Class '37' Nos 37098 and 37010 pass under the minor road leading from the town to the moor with a stone train. *TG*

There is an excellent museum of Dartmoor life in Okehampton town centre, with much to interest the industrial archaeologist and the naturalist. From Okehampton the Tarka Trail follows the route of the Two Museums Walk, the second museum being that of the Finch Foundry at Sticklepath. The Trail and railway part company at Fartherford Viaduct, the former heading for Belstone village and the latter Belstone Corner. There was a station at Belstone Corner, later renamed Sampford Courtenay after the village about 2 miles further north. Belstone Corner was remodelled to accommodate a railway bridge, and what was a straightforward crossroads became staggered, an interesting comparison with recent events at Mortehoe & Woolacombe station (see pages 74-5). From Belstone the Trail picks up the River Taw and turns north after Sticklepath.

Top and above **The Trail passes almost under the Fartherford Viaduct, shown here in 1912. The viaduct is now virtually hidden from view by trees, but there are a few clearings between the railway and the bypass.** *Beaford Archive/TG*

Left **Little is left of Sampford Courtenay station, other than the platforms and a small waiting shelter on the down side. A Class '37' takes a train load of ballast to Exeter Riverside on 2 July 1993.** *TG*

Tarka Trail and railway meet for the last time near the site of North Tawton station. Local trains originating from Exeter Central and two through trains per day from London stopped here, but patronage was always light. In common with Sampford Courtenay, the village was some distance to the north. 'Battle of Britain' Class No 34078 *222 Squadron* has just stopped with an Exeter to Padstow train.

The station buildings and goods yard are now in private hands, and the track has been singled and raised to platform level. *R. C. Riley/ TG*

Plan of North Tawton station in 1904. *Courtesy Okehampton Museum of Dartmoor Life*

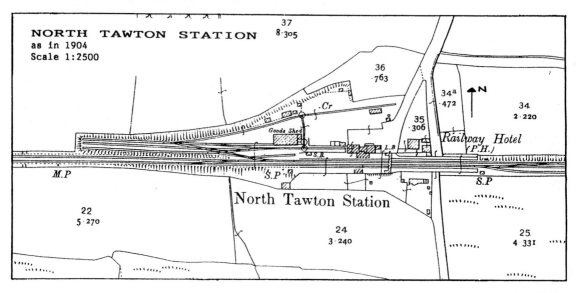

NORTH TAWTON STATION
as in 1904
Scale 1:2500

North Tawton Station

After passing under the railway the Trail continues close to the River Taw, which skirts North Tawton town. Two large factories dominate North Tawton, one old and virtually abandoned and the other built only a few years ago. The former was a woollen mill; many of the original buildings seen in this early view were replaced, and these are now themselves mostly unused. The modern factory in the background belongs to Express Foods. The two views were taken from the nearby hill. *Beaford Archive/TG*

The Trail continues north beyond North Tawton, closely following the River Taw until eventually Chenson Crossing is reached once more (see page 24). The traveller is thus back at the 'Tarka Line' between Exeter and Barnstaple, and in a further 2 miles Eggesford station is reached. The choice is between catching the train into Barnstaple or travelling south-east to Exeter, perhaps returning to Tarka Country in another season.

BIBLIOGRAPHY

Transport

Around the Branch Lines, Volume 1, Terry Gough (Oxford Publishing Company, 1982)
    ISBN 86093 159 5
Back Along the Lines, Victor Thompson (Badger Books, 1983) ISBN 0 946290 03 0
The Barnstaple and Ilfracombe Railway, Colin G. Maggs (Oakwood Press, 1988)
    ISBN 0 85361 368 0
The Bideford, Westward Ho! & Appledore Railway, Julia and Jonathan Baxter
    (H. J. Chard & Sons) ISBN 0 9507330 1 6
The Bideford, Westward Ho! & Appledore Railway, Stanley C. Jenkins (Oakwood Press, 1993)
    ISBN 0 85361 452 0
Branch Line to Lynton, Vic Mitchell and Keith Smith (Middleton Press, 1992) ISBN 1 873793 0 49
Branch Lines to Torrington, Vic Mitchell and Keith Smith (Middleton Press, 1994)
    ISBN 1 873793 37 5
British Roads Past and Present: Devon, Valerie R. Belsey (Past and Present, 1993)
    ISBN 1 85895 0007
Cross Country Routes of the Southern, Terry Gough (Oxford Publishing Company, 1983)
    ISBN 0 86093 267 2
Devon and Cornwall Railways in Old Photographs, Kevin Robertson (Alan Sutton, 1989)
    ISBN 0 86299 667 8
Exeter to Barnstaple, Vic Mitchell and Keith Smith (Middleton Press, 1993) ISBN 1 873793 1 5 4
The Kingdom by the Sea, Paul Theroux (Penguin, 1984) ISBN 0 14 007181 4
Lines to Torrington, John Nicholas (Oxford Publishing Company, 1984) ISBN 0 86093 145 5
LSWR West Country Lines Then and Now, Mac Hawkins (David and Charles, 1993)
    ISBN 0 7153 0122 5
The Lynton and Barnstaple Railway, L. T. Catchpole (Oakwood Press, 1988) ISBN 085361 363 X
The Lynton and Barnstaple Railway, G. A. Brown, J. D. C. Prideaux and H. G. Radcliffe
    (David and Charles, 1971)
The Lynton and Barnstaple Railway Album, J. D. C. A. Prideaux (David and Charles, 1974)
The North Devon Line, John Nicholas (Oxford Publishing Company, 1992) ISBN 0 86093 461 6
The North Devon and Cornwall Junction Light Railway, C. F. D. Whetmath and Douglas Stuckey
    (Forge Books, 1980)
Railway Landmarks in Devon, Jean Hall (David and Charles, 1982) ISBN 0 7153 8363 9
Railway World Special - The Southern West of Exeter, Peter Semmens (Ian Allan, 1988)
    ISBN 0 7110 1806 5
A Regional History of the Railways of Great Britain, Volume I: The West Country,
    David St John Thomas (David and Charles, 1981) ISBN 0 7153 8210 1
The Southern West of Salisbury, Terry Gough (Oxford Publishing Company, 1984)
    ISBN 0 86093 341 5
Take Off from Chivenor, Lois Lamplugh (Maslands Ltd, 1990) ISBN 0 946290 21 0
Walking West Country Railways, Christopher Somerville (David and Charles, 1982)
    ISBN 0 7153 8143 1
The Withered Arm, T. W. E. Roche (Forge Books, 1977)

Ordnance Survey Maps

First Edition (approx 1880): sheets 74, 82, reprinted by David and Charles, 1970
Popular Edition (approx 1918): sheets 118, 127, 128, 137
New Popular Edition (approx 1940): sheets 163, 175, 176
Landranger Series (current): sheets 180, 191

Town and Country

Barnstaple and North West Devon (Fifteenth Edition, Ward Lock, 1952)
Barnstaple, Town on the Taw, Lois Lamplugh (Phillimore, 1983)
Barnstaple Yesterday, Julia Barnes and Jonathan Baxter (Robert and Young, 1992)
Braunton, Tina Gaydon (Badger, 1989) ISBN 0946 29020 2
Changing Devon, James Derounian, Chris Smith and Chris Chapman (Tabb House Ltd, 1988)
Devon Town Trails, Peter Hunt and Marilyn Wills (Devon Books, 1988)
Exploring Barnstaple, John Bradbeer (Thematic Books, 1990) ISBN 0 948444 177
Exploring Bideford, Peter Christine (Thematic Books, 1989) ISBN 0 948444 169
Fremington Village and Pill, J. D. Collins, 1992
A History of Ilfracombe, Lois Lamplugh (Phillimore, 1984) ISBN 0 85033 525 6
Ilfracombe, A Pictoral Record, Glenn K. Horridge (Ammonite Books, 1986) ISBN 1 869866 00 2
Ilfracombe's Yesterdays, Lilian Wilson (Adrienne and Peter Oldale, 1976)
Instow Town and Old Yelland, J. D. Collins, 1992
The Lyn in Flood, Peter Keene and Derek Elsom (Thematic Books, 1990) ISBN 0948444 20 07
The Lynmouth Flood Disaster, Eric R. Delderfield (ERD, 1953) ISBN 0 900345 00 4
Market Towns of North Devon, Rosemary Anne Lauder (Badger Books, 1983) ISBN 0 946290 04 0
North Devon Country in Old Photographs (Parts I and II), Beryl Yates (Alan Sutton, 1989)
    ISBNs 0 86299 652X, 0 86299 727 5
North Devon Coast in Old Photographs, Beryl Yates (Alan Sutton, 1989) ISBN 0 86299 653 8
Picture Postcard Braunton, Bob Davis (Robert and Young, 1993) No ISBN
*Postcard Views of North Devon, Volume I (Ilfracombe), Volume II (Barnstaple),
    Volume III (South Molton)*, Tom Bartlett (Badger Books)
A Tale of Two Rivers, Rosemary Anne Lauder (1985) ISBN 0 946 290 11 3
Tarka Country, Trevor Beer (Badger Books, 1983) ISBN 0 946 290 059
The Tarka Trail, A Walker's Guide, produced by the Tarka Project (Devon Books, 1992)
    ISBN 0 86114 8770 0
Valley of the Rocks, Lynton, Peter Keene and Brian Pearce (Thematic Books, 1993)
    ISBN 0 948 444 25 8
Vanished Houses of North Devon, Rosemary Anne Lauder (North Devon Books, 1981)
    ISBN 0 9507920 04
Vanished Landmarks of North Devon, Rosemary Lauder (North Devon Books)
    ISBN 0 946 290 237
A Visitor's Guide to Devon, Brian Le Messurier (Moorland Publishing, 1983)
Woody Bay, Harriet Bridle (Merlin Books, 1991) ISBN 0 86303 510 8

INDEX OF LOCATIONS

Other titles of interest from Past & Present . . .